"A must-read for grantmakers…"

Praise for *Community Visions, Community Solutions*

"A must-read for grantmakers, individual donors, or any philanthropic professionals who hope to see community change in their lifetime."

Elwood Hopkins, Director, Los Angeles Urban Funders, Los Angeles, CA

"Community problems require comprehensive, integrated, sequential, and sustained approaches that will improve systems. Funders, however, continue their fragmented 'silver-bullet' responses. The questions raised in this book will be useful to any foundation that hopes to increase the effectiveness of its resource allocations, whether or not that leads to collaboration. Any leader, whether in a foundation, a nonprofit organization, or a public agency, should read this book and ponder 'what might be' in more effective community problem solving. A very useful addition to the literature."

Eugene Wilson, Senior Vice President, Ewing Marion Kauffman Foundation, Kansas City, MO

"As funders attempt to enhance the community's problem-solving capacity, services integration, and human and financial resources coordination, this book will be invaluable. It offers a litany of best practices for achieving these enhancements within an era of enormous social and technology changes."

Paula Allen-Meares, Dean and Professor, Norma Radin Collegiate Professor of Social Work, University of Michigan School of Social Work, Ann Arbor, MI

"Funders and other community leaders can and should solve problems—by using collaboration as a tool, releasing the highest aspirations of the group, and remaining open to new ideas. Authors Connor and Kadel-Taras help funders understand the dynamics and the process of community problem solving and become a responsible part of the solution. Their examples of funders' experiences, their focus on solutions, and their 'prompts' on how to 'get there' are especially helpful. A great tool for funders who want to take a role in solving community problems at the most comprehensive level."

Richard K. Rappleye, Vice President, Field Services, C.S. Mott Foundation, Flint, MI

"In a clear and concise manner, *Community Visions, Community Solutions* helps funders look at investing in a new way for more impact. This book can help foundations examine their policies and procedures as a stimulus for doing business in an enlightened twenty-first century style."

Patricia Deinhart, Community Liaison, Northwest Area Foundation, Saint Paul, MN

"This book provides a compelling approach for how funders can be more deliberately involved in creating collaboration and community problem solving."

Dahnesh Medora, Director of External Relations and Research, The Tides Center, San Francisco, CA

A FUNDER'S GUIDE
from **WILDER & GEO**

Community Visions, Community Solutions: Grantmaking for Comprehensive Impact is one of a series of works published by Amherst H. Wilder Foundation in collaboration with Grantmakers for Effective Organizations (GEO). Together, we hope to strengthen nonprofit organizations, the communities they serve, and the nonprofit sector by helping grantmakers in their work with nonprofits. Other titles in the series include:

Strengthening Nonprofit Performance: A Funder's Guide to Capacity Building

The Amherst H. Wilder Foundation is one of the largest and oldest endowed human service and community development organizations in the United States. For more than ninety years, the Wilder Foundation has been providing health and human services that help children and families grow strong, the elderly age with dignity, and the community grow in its ability to meet its own needs.

We hope you find this book helpful! Should you need information about our consulting services, please contact:

Wilder Center for Communities
Amherst H. Wilder Foundation
919 Lafond Avenue
Saint Paul, MN 55104
651-642-4022

For more information about other Wilder Foundation publications, please see the back of this book or contact:

Wilder Publishing Center
Amherst H. Wilder Foundation
919 Lafond Avenue
Saint Paul, MN 55104
800-274-6024
www.wilder.org/pubs

To learn more about the Collaboratory for Community Support, contact:

The Collaboratory for Community Support
2410 Newport Road
Ann Arbor, MI 48103
734-623-4952
www.comnet.org/collaboratorycs/

Edited by Vincent Hyman and Judith Peacock

Book design by Mighty Media, Minneapolis, MN
 Text and cover design: Chris Long
 Illustrations: Michael Bonilla

Manufactured in the United States of America

Second printing, November 2004

Library of Congress Cataloging-in-Publication Data

Connor, Joseph A., 1952–

  Community visions, community solutions : grantmaking for comprehensive impact / by Joseph A. Connor and Stephanie Kadel-Taras.

     p.   cm.

Includes bibliographical references and index.

  ISBN 0-940069-30-X (pbk.)

1. Community organization--United States. 2. Public-private sector cooperation--United States. 3. Social service--United States. I. Kadel-Taras, Stephanie. II. Title.

HM766 .C67 2003

361.8'0973--dc21

                                                              2002153040

Printed on recycled paper. 10% postconsumer waste.

Community Visions, Community Solutions:
Grantmaking for Comprehensive Impact

by Joseph A. Connor and Stephanie Kadel-Taras

Community Visions, Community Solutions:
Grantmaking for Comprehensive Impact

by Joseph A. Connor and Stephanie Kadel-Taras

AMHERST H.
WILDER
FOUNDATION

SAINT PAUL,
MINNESOTA

We thank The David and Lucile Packard Foundation and the Amherst H. Wilder Foundation
for support of this publication.

The Amherst H. Wilder Foundation is one of the largest and oldest endowed human service and community development organizations in the United States. For more than ninety years, the Wilder Foundation has been providing health and human services that help children and families grow strong, the elderly age with dignity, and the community grow in its ability to meet its own needs.

We hope you find this book helpful! Should you need information about our consulting services, please contact:

Wilder Center for Communities
Amherst H. Wilder Foundation
919 Lafond Avenue
Saint Paul, MN 55104
651-642-4022

For more information about other Wilder Foundation publications, please see the back of this book or contact:

Wilder Publishing Center
Amherst H. Wilder Foundation
919 Lafond Avenue
Saint Paul, MN 55104
800-274-6024
www.wilder.org/pubs

To learn more about the Collaboratory for Community Support, contact:

The Collaboratory for Community Support
2410 Newport Road
Ann Arbor, MI 48103
734-623-4952
www.comnet.org/collaboratorycs/

Edited by Vincent Hyman and Judith Peacock

Book design by Mighty Media, Minneapolis, MN
  Text and cover design: Chris Long
  Illustrations: Michael Bonilla

Manufactured in the United States of America

First printing January 2003

Library of Congress Cataloging-in-Publication Data

Connor, Joseph A., 1952–

  Community visions, community solutions : grantmaking for comprehensive impact / by Joseph A. Connor and Stephanie Kadel-Taras.

      p.   cm.

Includes bibliographical references and index.

  ISBN 0-940069-30-X (pbk.)

1. Community organization--United States. 2. Public-private sector cooperation--United States. 3. Social service--United States. I. Kadel-Taras, Stephanie. II. Title.

HM766 .C67 2003

361.8'0973--dc21

                                                                    2002153040

Printed on recycled paper. 10% postconsumer waste.

Dedication

To my three children—Jessica, Kerianne, and Patrick—who fuel my passion for a future of successful communities.

JOSEPH A. CONNOR

To Nellie A. Thompson, who regularly reminds me why the systems need to change and why every resident is a treasure not to be wasted.

STEPHANIE KADEL-TARAS

About the Authors

Joseph A. "Jay" Connor is the founder and CEO of the Collaboratory for Community Support. He has extensive leadership experience in the business, nonprofit, and public policy arenas. His major interest is in crossing the borders between these sectors. His unique background provides a framework from which to draw solutions and perspective on the major issues that confront U.S. communities. He is a sought-after speaker and consultant.

Before founding the Collaboratory, Jay was president and CEO of Nonprofit Enterprise at Work (NEW), a nonprofit management support organization in Ann Arbor, Michigan. Jay also has more than twenty years of experience in senior business management at Fortune 100 companies. In addition to his professional commitments, Jay has been an active volunteer and community leader. He sits on the advisory board for Crain's Nonprofit News and is a member of the McAdam Book Award Committee, which recognizes the best book published in the nonprofit field each year.

Jay holds a J.D. and an M.B.A. in management from Northwestern University. He is an adjunct professor at the University of Michigan, where he teaches graduate students from the schools of Urban Planning, Business, Public Policy, and Social Work.

STEPHANIE KADEL-TARAS, director of research and publications for the Collaboratory, has more than twelve years of experience in research, writing, and management in nonprofit and government organizations in Florida, New York, and Michigan. She has also served as director of education at Nonprofit Enterprise at Work.

Stephanie has always emphasized the value of well-organized information and "usable research" for community decision making. She is skilled at synthesizing and drawing practical recommendations from complex, multi-disciplinary knowledge and ideas. With more than twenty publications to her credit, Stephanie has written nationally-acclaimed guidebooks and articles on such topics as social services integration, systemic change, and school restructuring. She also writes a monthly column for a local Ann Arbor magazine and volunteers as an adult literacy tutor. Stephanie holds a Ph.D. in education and sociology from Syracuse University and an M.A. in educational foundations and policy from the University of Michigan.

Acknowledgments

As with community problem solving, the writing of a book can't be accomplished without plenty of behind-the-scenes help. We would like to thank individuals at the Annie E. Casey Foundation, James Irvine Foundation, Ewing Marion Kauffman Foundation, John S. and James L. Knight Foundation, Charles Stewart Mott Foundation, Northwest Area Foundation, Peninsula Community Foundation, and Copeland Fund of the Pittsburgh Community Foundation for their participation in the research for this book. Additional contributions to the research came from interviews with leaders at the Community Council of Greater Dallas, Community Services Planning Council (Sacramento), DC Agenda, Jacksonville Community Council, Kansas City LINC, Los Angeles Urban Funders, National Association of Planning Councils, Northern California Council for the Community, Peninsula Partnership for Children, Youth, and Families, and Urban Strategies Council (Oakland). Further insights for our work were gained through interactions with the W. K. Kellogg Foundation, the Surdna Foundation, Gary MacDougal (former chair of Illinois Governor's Task Force on Human Services Reform), Gary Stangler (former director of Missouri Department of Social Services), and many fine individuals in communities throughout North America. Also, our ongoing relationship with the Amherst H. Wilder Foundation continues to inform our work.

We are grateful for the hands-on research assistance provided by Richard Beaman, Christina Harley Ventrelle, Rukshan Fernando, Megan Schatz, and Allison Suter. Many other professional colleagues, too numerous to name, have encouraged us with a listening ear and careful reviews of our work, including those at the University of Michigan and Washtenaw County government.

We wish to thank the following people whose thoughtful critiques of our first draft guided the final development of this book:

Patricia Deinhart	Richard K. Rappleye
Paul Fate	Frank J. Schweigert
Elwood Hopkins	Miriam Shark
Carol Lukas	Diane K. Vinokur
Dahnesh Medora	Eugene Wilson
Jane Moore	

Most importantly, we couldn't have done without the daily engagement and insights of our most valuable colleague and friend, Patricia Denig. And we are forever grateful to our spouses, Carol Connor and Jeff Taras, who are great community contributors in their own ways. Finally, this book would not have been possible without the generous support of the Power Foundation of Philip and Kathy Power and the Board of the Collaboratory for Community Support.

Contents

Introduction

THIS BOOK IS ABOUT HOW COMMUNITIES CAN SOLVE PROBLEMS. To paraphrase Vince Lombardi, solutions are everything. Solutions attract energy, engagement, and enthusiasm. They have the power to transform frustrating, thankless tasks into the creative currency of community change. Whatever work being done in the name of philanthropy or charity or social improvement should be assessed as to how it moves a community to solutions. Programs, agencies, initiatives, and collaborations are the building blocks of solutions—not ends in themselves. They should exist only to lead to solutions. This book is about uncovering the community's highest aspirations for itself and its residents, and supporting and sustaining the systemic, strategic efforts to get to desired solutions.

The convergence of recent trends is making problem solving more feasible for local communities today:

- Government devolution has given much of the decision-making power to the local level for how money is spent and policies are implemented.

- Advances in information technology have expanded people's ability to work together, share data, identify trends, track outcomes, and make informed decisions.

- An ongoing blurring of the nonprofit, for-profit, and government sectors has increased opportunities to take full advantage of all the community's resources to tackle complex problems.

In short, the solutions that communities want can be achieved with better alignment of goals, resources, and information, and this alignment is more possible now than ever before.

Thus, this book is also about collaboration, but only because community problem solving requires community members to work together. This is not meant to be another collaboration guidebook, with all the careful definitions of group work and suggestions for how to collaborate effectively. Everyone knows what good collaboration requires—a shared vision, mutual respect, clear roles, open communication. Yet, as seen time and again in communities, knowing the value of collaboration and instituting the internal mechanisms for good group work do not necessarily mean that the collaboration will lead to results. While community members are spending more time in collaborative meetings, they are often seeing little change in the way work is organized to reach solutions. The outcomes of their efforts simply do not match the passion they bring to the work. Plans stall; progress drifts; trust erodes; commitment falters.

Such disappointing results often stem from a lack of attention to the ultimate reason to collaborate: solving community problems. Just as we want communities to focus more on solutions, so we also devote most of this book to strategies for reaching the community's highest aspirations. And while the strategies presented here still rely heavily on collaboration as a tool, we want to be clear up front that we do not value collaboration as an end in itself, nor do we specifically advocate for collaboration in order to reduce duplication of services and programs.

Disappointing results often stem from a lack of attention to the ultimate reason to collaborate: solving community problems.

In fact, our experience working with collaborative groups leaves us concerned that people have become suspicious of collaboration as simply a method to identify and weed out "unnecessary" organizations. If participants perceive that the primary purpose of collaboration is to reduce the number of organizations working on a problem (and hence the number of hungry mouths calling to foundations for support), those who feel their own work threatened will be less likely to become fully engaged.

If, however, collaboration is practiced as a means to reach solutions, and participants perceive this as the genuine goal, then a variety of options remain open for consideration. Efficiency may not take the form of fewer organizations, but may instead result from communicating better, streamlining more processes, getting the job done right the first time around, and staying focused on the desired goal. Communities may find that preserving multiple organizations with multiple strategies is more desirable than consolidating and reducing duplication. Or, in the end, maybe they won't, and some organizations will find that their work is no longer needed. But regardless of the tactics chosen, the purpose of the collaboration remains clear: figuring out how the community can organize its work and resources in the most effective and efficient way to solve problems. The challenge becomes how to organize and support collaboration (even among seemingly unnatural partners) so that solutions can be reached.

This book is about how funders can help communities meet this challenge. We've written this book primarily for funders, because funders often serve as a catalyst for community change, and many of the strategies for solving problems require new ways of using resources. However, the issues and strategies discussed are also relevant to the work of many community leaders and daily service providers who may find here some solutions to their challenges—and ideas to present to their funding organizations.

When we talk about "funders," we are referring to private funding organizations of all kinds, including community foundations, family foundations, local United Way organizations, national foundations, corporate foundations, and private donors. Although this concept encompasses a wide range of funders, and each reader will have to adapt the ideas to his or her own organization's unique characteristics, we believe that the messages apply across all private funding organizations that are concerned about solving community problems in North America.*

We will begin by exploring why funders are often frustrated in their efforts to positively improve communities, and why many collaborations have so far failed to live up to their promises. Then we will discuss new approaches to funding and highlight the value of supportive services for successful community problem solving.

* While many of the lessons discussed in this book also apply to government funding, the implementation of new approaches in the policy arena will require a different set of strategies.

The discussions and suggestions presented here are based on five years of research and hands-on community work. We have explored these ideas through interviews of, presentations to, and discussions with staff in national, regional, and community foundations around the country. We have also refined our thinking through invaluable interactions with hundreds of community leaders from places as diverse as San Francisco, Fort Worth, Battle Creek, Pittsburgh, Minneapolis, and Calgary. We draw from recent literature on philanthropy and community change, case studies of community organizations, and direct experience with collaborative projects in several communities in the United States and Canada. Having tried to make sense of our learning by writing this book, we hope you will find that it provokes both thought and action, that it fosters new ideas, and that it leads to solutions.

Funder Frustration:
Having an Impact

"IF I HAD KNOWN IT WOULD COME TO THIS, I NEVER WOULD HAVE entered the field." We heard this from the president of a large local funding organization in a major metropolitan area. This was the first time we had met her, and her honesty was unexpected and disheartening, yet all too familiar. Here, in one brief exclamation, she had crystallized the essence of hundreds of conversations we've had with funders and nonprofit leaders over the past several years.

For many such committed and hardworking individuals, the days are filled with activities that fail to approach the vision of community and societal impact that propelled them along this career path. One veteran grantmaker and vice president of a major foundation even told us he was hard put to find successes in his work: "I can tell you an awful lot about experiences, but when you try to get complex social dynamics like we deal with to be comprehensive, integrated, sequential, and sustained for lasting impact, it's tough."

In our conversations with funders, it was clear that they simply want what communities want: a positive impact on the problem. Whether you call it

"When you try to get complex social dynamics to be comprehensive, integrated, sequential, and sustained for lasting impact, it's tough."

"success" or "effectiveness" or "outcomes" or "making a difference," the whole point of giving dollars—the main reason for the existence of the funding organization—is to have a positive impact, to get to solutions. But even when a funder has moved from programmatic, categorical support to integrated approaches with broad community engagement and intensive collaboration, the funder often continues to be frustrated. Says one foundation leader with years of experience supporting community-based efforts:

> If you looked across all of those [initiatives we'd funded] and you said, "Are we moving the needle for the kids who are most at risk for being left behind?" you had to answer "Nope." We really felt that we, and others in the field, were accomplishing many things, but were falling short on three: impact, durability, and scale.

Reasons abound for why problems don't get solved and why funders' contributions and hard work still lead to frustration, but our emphasis in this book is to get beyond the problems to focus on solutions. So we will briefly highlight a few issues that get in the way of success:

- Fractured problems, fractured resources
- Fractured outcomes
- The power dilemma
- The cloak of collaboration

Fractured Problems, Fractured Resources

In the ongoing endeavor to solve complex, interwoven problems, funders, nonprofits, and community leaders all face the same uncertainties: no clear definitions of success, difficulties documenting improvements, and no marketlike forces to guide decision making. Funders (both private and public) have traditionally responded to these uncertainties by dividing complex problems into separate issues, categories, and funding pots. This allows foundations to target their resources carefully, dig deeply into only a few issues, and find their niche in the larger field of philanthropy. It also allows them to manage their funds in an orderly way as they divide up tasks, institute a clear process for reviewing requests, and avoid being swamped by proposals for everything under the sun.

Just as funders take a fragmented approach to grantmaking, nonprofit organizations take a similar approach to services. Whether through their own design, or as a response to funding opportunities, nonprofits have created multiple and separate problem-solving efforts, leaving the community as a whole all but forgotten, as illustrated in Figure 1, Fractured Resources and Silo Efforts, on page 8. Social problem solving in communities ends up divided into uncoordinated, piecemeal services that are nearly impossible to enumerate, navigate, or evaluate. Researcher John O'Looney estimates that a single midsize community (population of 100,000 to 250,000) has 400 to 500 social services programs (let alone environmental, cultural, and other services). It took him six months to map out all the services available to youth with emotional and behavioral problems in the state of Georgia, and he ended up with an incomprehensible (and still incomplete) drawing.[1]

There have been good reasons for looking more at the parts than the whole and for specializing in a narrowly defined set of problems. This approach has enabled funders and nonprofits to study the details of an issue and refine their expertise on particular matters. Universities, public policy institutions, and health care providers have all elevated the role of the specialist throughout the second half of the twentieth century. Like the naturalist who worries about rain forest destruction but spends most of her time studying endangered poison-dart frogs, funders and their grantees have understandably specialized, taking on a smaller piece of a complex problem as one doorway into the issues.

Figure 1. Fractured Resources and Silo Efforts

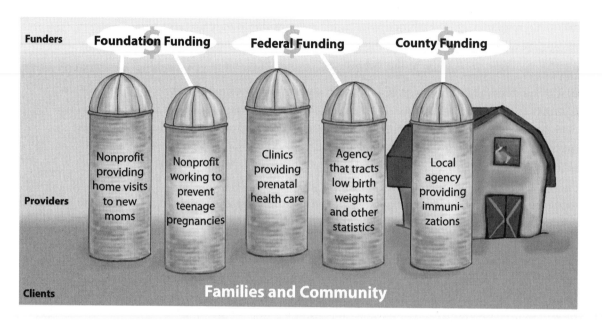

Social problem solving has evolved into a collection of piecemeal, often uncoordinated services, as shown in this figure. Here each "silo" has a separate part of the solution to improve prenatal and infant care.

Fragmentation of funding and services has also resulted from funders and communities trying to take immediate action on suddenly more noticeable and severe problems. When hunger, homelessness, child abuse, or toxic waste caught people's collective attention, programs sprang up to address the specific need. Problems were often narrowly defined and advocacy narrowly targeted to the individual person or particular location. Moments of crisis needed immediate action, but these responses were not seen in the context of broad social issues and systems.

The effort that funders and communities have spent trying to make sense of and address discrete problems has been valuable. But the time has now come to pull back from the details and concentrate resources and effort more on the whole. Now that scientists have a better sense of how the elements of a rain forest work, they are necessarily focusing on conservation of the entire ecosystem—plants, animals, water, and human residents together.

Similarly, funders and communities can no longer afford to continue fracturing problems and funding into separate specialties. After valuable years of study and work on the pieces of the problem of homelessness, communities now recognize that they cannot end homelessness without addressing all the root causes simultaneously and in a coordinated manner: substance abuse, mental illness, domestic violence, lack of affordable housing, and lack of living-wage jobs for underskilled residents. Fortunately, from previous work, communities understand more about each of these challenges than ever before. But if they are now going to bring the specialized knowledge and services together to address the whole, they need foundations that are also prepared to support work on the whole problem. So far, few foundations that support homeless shelters also support economic development; few foundations that support women and children's issues also support mental health services. Or when a funder does have programs for each of these problems, it may not have the internal mechanisms to process funding requests that intertwine these issues.

Of course, foundations aren't the only ones who respond to the complexity and uncertainty of community problem solving with piecemeal grantmaking. Federal, state, and local governments—in both their policy making and funding allocations—take the same approach, often for the same fundamental reasons. One might argue, in fact, that foundations are often simply responding to the environment of fragmentation resulting from government mandates as they look for ways to enhance resources for the community's work.

The time has now come to pull back from the details and concentrate resources and effort more on the whole.

At the same time, nonprofits also play their part in encouraging fractured funding. While funding availability often dictates nonprofit actions, nonprofit specialization and requests for funding can help define how funders establish their priorities. All the players in the field of social change have participated in the segmenting of problems and of the resources to address them. But funders can now take up a leadership role in putting the pieces back together and helping everyone focus on the whole.

While the first response to this fracturing has been a call for mergers and consolidations to reduce duplication, this approach may jeopardize the search for solutions.[2] Funders and communities should begin by looking at the details of these services and explore where multiple strategies in diverse locations are, in fact, valuable to solving the problem. The goal, after all, is fewer people experiencing homelessness or fewer emotional and behavioral problems in youth; the goal is not fewer programs. Of course, the choices and access points need to be made more visible for clients, and the services no doubt need to be coordinated to provide comprehensive assistance to families; these efforts may then lead to fewer programs. But this is where collaboration to reduce fragmented work becomes valuable: to help communities figure out how to harness their resources to address the whole problem and achieve solutions.

Fractured Outcomes

A further challenge to solving whole problems at the community-wide level is measuring outcomes. The fragmented systems created for addressing community problems are essentially lacking in feedback loops. With piecemeal approaches and without the right indicators, research, and technology to measure results, it's hard to know when or how clients' needs are being met or the community is benefiting. As Patricia Stonesifer of the Bill and Melinda Gates Foundation said, "It would be possible to blow $100 billion" and have no impact at all.[3]

Funders are disquieted by the possibility of having no impact, and they are justifiably concerned about being perceived that way by others. Consider, for example, the critical press accompanying a report on the Annenberg Foundation's $500 million grant to eighteen public school systems. The report suggested that the money essentially left the systems unchanged and "didn't accomplish what the Annenberg Foundation had hoped."[4] While this conclusion is questionable, the attention it got was surely embarrassing for the foundation. And the widely varied opinions that later surfaced about whether or not the Annenberg Foundation grant had positively affected the schools simply point to the difficulty of measuring the results of community work and the impact of foundation grants.

To respond to the problem of measuring impact, the nonprofit, philanthropic, and government sectors have turned to "outcomes" evaluation. This is a step forward from previous approaches to evaluation, which simply counted activities—the number of people attending a job-training class, the percentage of county land set aside for parks, the number of kids participating in an after-school arts program. Recognizing that these tallies do not tell much about whether services are changing people's lives for the better, funders have begun to request that their grantees provide them with measurements of the outcomes achieved—the attitudes and behaviors that change as a result of grantee services, not just who uses the services.

But even with these improvements in evaluation, the outcomes that would indicate successful solutions to community problems are often bigger than most organizations by themselves can reach or measure. While a community may want healthy children, it can only measure progress toward this goal by measuring separate programs and discrete outcomes—numbers of immunizations, parents who report serving healthier meals after taking a nutrition class, the percentage increase in kids exercising regularly, stronger antismoking attitudes among elementary school students, and so on. Only when the community looks at *all* of these programs and outcomes together can it get a sense of the progress being made toward more healthy young lives. But when the grants and the services are fractured, the outcomes become inherently fractured, and people rarely see the whole picture. In a system of fragmented services and multiple strategies, meaningful outcomes must be looked at across organizations, at the systemic and community level.

The Power Dilemma

As funders wrestle with the problems of fractured services and outcomes at the local level, they quickly encounter a dilemma regarding their role in communities and who should hold the power to change things. Although foundations account for just 10 percent of giving to the nonprofit sector, their grants can set the agenda for how issues will be addressed.[5] The topics that interest them, the organizations they fund, the speeches and articles they publish, and the approaches they label as innovative are closely watched by nonprofit and community leaders.

As a senior executive at one national foundation points out:

> We've recognized that leading with money turns out to be a mistake—you put enough zeros after the one and you get anybody in any community to say, "Yep, whatever it is you're selling we agree. (Forget what we think is really going on in our town and forget what we think are really the strengths and challenges we face, we'll just tell you whatever you need to hear so you'll send the check.)"

The requirements that funders attach to their grants can have a significant effect on the way the grantees address a problem. For instance, before the California Wellness Foundation would give money to comprehensive teenage pregnancy prevention, it required community applicants to recognize and respond to the fact that some teens are sexually active. As a result, whatever strategies the community implemented had to include contraceptive services. In contrast, when the Colorado Trust gave grants to five communities for collaboration to address teen pregnancy, one of its requirements was that each community reach consensus about what to do. As a result, none of the communities ended up offering contraceptive services, because none could come to consensus around that issue.[6] Thus, two funders, tackling the same problem with different requirements, elicited very different—nearly opposite—responses from the communities.

The power that grant dollars have over nonprofit and community work creates painful dilemmas for funders. Many funders (especially nonlocal foundations) hesitate to set parameters, provide too much guidance, or delineate expectations of their grantees for fear of being perceived as imposing their own agenda or taking control of the community's work. Research and experience today emphasize that ideas which emerge from within the community are more likely to take hold than those which are perceived as imposed from elsewhere. Funders, thus, take stances such as the following, which come from two foundations with different priorities:

> We're not pushing. We're trying to be respectful of communities in terms of where they are, what they think they need, what the local leadership is calling for.

> We don't try to impose anything on those organizations; they have to come to it themselves. We can guide local neighborhood associations to other places, but we can't push this stuff—it has to be pulled by them.

This approach to grantmaking grows out of a much improved understanding in U.S. society of the diversity of the population, the rights of citizens, the need for everyone's voice to be heard, and the lessons history teaches about how those with power (money, influence, white skin) have taken advantage of those without power. As another foundation leader points out, "The people who are in the boardrooms of philanthropy, by and large, have résumés that are similar to one another, and they are not the résumés of the people in the community."

The power that grant dollars have over nonprofit and community work creates painful dilemmas for funders.

The philanthropic sector, cognizant of these issues, is striving to uphold the values that come from respecting differences and empowering others. The challenge comes when the desire to empower prevents funders from taking action. The power dilemma can send funders too far in the other direction, as suggested by this observation from the president of the Minneapolis Foundation, Emmet Carson, in an opinion piece in the *Chronicle of Philanthropy*:

It is tantamount to an emergency medical team arriving at the scene of a serious traffic accident, running up to an injured pedestrian who is barely conscious, and saying: "Ma'am, we're going to empower you to save yourself, not that we're saying you have a problem. We're going to put this equipment that you have never seen before on the ground next to you and, if you choose, you may save yourself."[7]

As the wry humor here points out, communities simply don't have all the information and knowledge that would allow them to take the initiative and solve their problems on their own. Even if foundation money is promised to respond to their requests, waiting for solutions to bubble up from the grassroots without first infusing communities with best-practices ideas, statistical data, and collaboration tools may be more detrimental than the risk of imposition. Community members may assume that foundation staff know more than the community. This can intensify problems of trust between funders (who want to stay in the background) and grantees (who think funders aren't being forthcoming about their real agenda and what they know). Seesawing between these perspectives leaves communities frustrated and foundations in a power dilemma that only exacerbates the challenges of making a positive impact.

The Cloak of Collaboration

Almost nothing that we've discussed so far is news. Funders and nonprofits have been trying for several years to streamline funding, coordinate services, strengthen outcomes measures, and empower communities for change. Most funders today realize that collaboration in communities is necessary for impact, and they have supported everything from "service integration" to "interagency collaboration" to "comprehensive community initiatives." A recent study of nineteen major foundations concluded that funders recognize that "the interconnected problems of children, especially disadvantaged ones, require comprehensive solutions." Foundations have become frustrated with piecemeal approaches, says the report, and are now "concentrating many of their resources on long-term, comprehensive, place-based community strategies designed to improve outcomes."[8] This mirrors what we heard from a senior officer at one big-city foundation:

> This is the only way you can go. You can't continue to do silver-bullet, categorical approaches to these things. You have to be coordinated in both your public and private approaches to these tough problems.

But the more effort funders and communities make to collaborate, the more they seem to be frustrated. Even when participants have followed all the recent advice on how to collaborate, they find themselves stuck in the process, without the support, resources, information, and shared aspirations that are necessary for changing systems and solving problems. They end up agreeing with the county official in Minnesota who told researcher Melissa Stone, "Let's just declare collaboration a victory and get away from it."[9]

Such frustration, it seems to us, comes from a tendency for communities to don a cloak of collaboration without fundamentally changing the way they try to reach solutions. Collaboration is often undertaken primarily to obtain or share resources. Even when participants try to ground their collaborative efforts in aspirations for the community, they can be easily sidetracked by existing ways of working and influenced to shift their focus to simply trying to coordinate the programs they already have in place. The best interests of the community can be overshadowed by the desire to preserve established organizations. And plans of nonprofit leaders to engage businesses, religious institutions, schools, government, and neighborhood leaders begin to seem more complicated to nonprofit leaders than just trying to do the work themselves.

The lack of collaboration among funders may also prevent community leaders from aligning their goals and resources to reach their aspirations. Even as government agencies and foundations value collaboration, each wants to be identified with its own strategies, terminology, and grantees. Thus, when we convinced a dozen funders in one Midwest city (including the United Way, city government, county agencies, the community foundation, and a family foundation) to attend a meeting to talk about funding for homelessness, they wouldn't even entertain the idea of working together on the problem. Their response was to wait and see what the nonprofits decided to do, and then each of them might consider a grant request tailored to their funding process and priorities. Such a hesitancy among funders to model collaboration and community-wide visioning is frustrating for nonprofits, who may feel unfairly burdened by the challenges of collaboration ("If they don't have to do it, why should we?"), hampered by fragmentary funding in their desire to collaborate, hamstrung by unaligned reporting structures and outcomes measures, and condemned to operational constraints because of funders' unwillingness to sustain a shared commitment to solving the problem.

Of course, nonprofits themselves may be reluctant to do more than assume the appearance of collaboration. While they may embrace the message, "You should collaborate," they also hear another message, "You are in competition with each other for a piece of a small pie." Being told to collaborate and compete simultaneously is, to say the least, confusing for nonprofit leaders. Many nonprofit collaborations, therefore, do not lead to solutions that are greater than the sum of their parts, because each participating organization is concerned about protecting its own turf (of available funding and clients). When groups of nonprofits do explore how they might collaborate to address a problem, their goal and plans can end up as a least-common-denominator agreement about what to do, because the changes required for a grander vision are too risky in the larger competitive climate. In the current context, telling nonprofits to collaborate and expecting them to solve the community's problems is like sending two six-year-olds to the corner and telling them they can't come out until they get along. The most that the six-year-olds are going to do is focus on how to get out of the corner, not how to become best friends. Similarly, without the structures and resources that uphold collaboration, nonprofits by themselves can only take collaboration so far.

While U.S. businesses invest heavily in the services and people needed just to glue together their multibusiness alliances, nonprofits, funders, and communities make comparatively little investment in ensuring the success of collaboration to solve problems.[10] Perhaps they believe that collaboration should come naturally, so there's no reason to "artificially" support it. Or perhaps they simply haven't clearly identified how collaboration can be supported to get to solutions. The remainder of this book tries to bring clarity to this challenge.

Getting from Here to There

In summary, as funders seek to have a positive impact in communities, to encourage comprehensive, integrated solutions to social, environmental, and cultural problems, they continue to find it difficult to get new approaches off the ground. Funders and communities are weighed down by past ways of working—such as fragmented problems, fractured resources, uncoordinated public policies, and turf protection—that are no longer very helpful. And they are still discovering the promises and the puzzles associated with such tools as outcomes measurement, empowerment, and collaboration.

As the tools of information technology and government devolution are added to the mix, is it any wonder nobody knows how to fly this thing? It is both an exciting and scary time to fund community work, but we believe that by keeping one landmark in sight—solving community problems—the excitement will eventually overcome the fear. In the next chapters, we will explore a variety of practical strategies to help funders and communities get the successes and solutions they desire.

Strategies for Funding Solutions

FOSTERING SUCCESSFUL COMMUNITY PROBLEM SOLVING RE-quires funders to approach their grantmaking in fundamentally new ways. If funders want to solve problems, and if they recognize that this requires working together—not only across nonprofits but also all sectors of society—then the baseline responsibility for funders should be to enable communities to redesign how work is organized to reach solutions.

This chapter suggests ways funding organizations can help communities and nonprofits get beyond the piecemeal approaches, power struggles, and failed collaborations to reorganize work in local communities and attain the highest goals. We have organized these suggestions into three broad categories:

- *Fund Communities.* This section looks at the roles funders can play to help the community aspire, to encourage broad community engagement, and to ensure access to information for decision making.

- *Fund Systems.* This section explores the use of grant dollars to support service strategies, management information systems, governance, and outcomes measurement, all at the multiorganizational level.

- *Be the Change You Wish to See.* This section discusses making changes in the internal management and operation of funding organizations to support community problem solving.

Fund Communities

The first step toward fostering successful community problem solving is for funders to focus their giving on the work of communities—whether neighborhoods, towns, cities, or regions—not the work of programs. This means funding work at a systems level, crossing artificial boundaries of sectors and programs so community problems can be addressed in a comprehensive way.

To do this, funders will need to foster the processes of rallying community members around shared aspirations for the future and reorganizing community work to reach those aspirations. In practical terms, this means supporting community collaboration. But instead of turning to collaboration as a way to bring together multiple programs and to keep organizations abreast of each other's existing activities, communities will turn to collaboration as the method for developing shared goals and action plans. Then organization and programmatic efforts (some of which may need to be coordinated) will become the building blocks for attaining the goals.

This emphasis on community work speaks to respondents to a recent survey by the Pew Partnership for Civic Change, nearly 90 percent of whom agreed that "working in groups to solve problems takes more time, but works in the long run."[11] Funders who want to support this group work can turn to a wealth of learning that has resulted from various efforts at community building, community organizing, community development, systems reform, and comprehensive community initiatives.[12] These approaches range from recruiting residents to get involved in decision making, to training new local leaders, to building new collaborative infrastructure, to developing the capacity for teamwork, to engaging entire neighborhoods in plans to improve quality of life. While the success of these kinds of community work has been variable, we believe the opportunities to succeed have never been greater than now, with the convergence of technology, government devolution, and sector blurring.

How can this work be guided by practical actions of funders? Experience and research suggest several key responses:

- Help communities aspire
- Encourage broad community engagement
- Ensure information for community empowerment

Help communities aspire

Community work is challenging, time consuming, frustrating at times, and ever evolving. What makes the struggle worth it is the reason for doing it—the community's high aspirations for the future. Community members hunger for meaning in their mutual work; they want to be inspired. When they come together to reach a goal, their shared aspiration creates a kind of gravitational pull that brings in more people, more ideas, more hard work, and a lasting commitment. Funders can help communities aspire by funding the process of developing shared aspirations and the plans for reaching them.

When community members come together to reach a goal, their shared aspiration creates a kind of gravitational pull that brings in more people, more ideas, more hard work, and a lasting commitment.

Funders don't want to simply serve as the cash machine for the status quo. Before making grants, they should expect community members to explore the question, What do we want for our community and residents? In most cases, the answers to this question will lead to the need for multiple programs and community-wide collaboration, which will likely change who the grantees are and what strategies should be funded.

One of the first challenges to helping communities aspire, however, is that most communities lack a forum to even ask the question, What do we want? As the Center for the Study of Social Policy points out, "No entity is envisioned in current federal, state, or local policy as the place where diverse

Opportunities for Funders to Help Communities Aspire

- Ask the question, What does our community want?
- Help identify a local forum to discuss the community's aspirations.
- Support the convening and regular meeting of a broad spectrum of members of the community.
- Challenge community members to keep their aspirations at the forefront of their planning.
- Participate as a member of the community in the visioning and planning.
- Provide "political cover" for others.
- Behave as a servant-leader by enabling others to succeed and take the credit.

programs fit within a *unified community strategy* that could accomplish clearly defined results" [our emphasis].[13] Funders can play a crucial role in filling this gap in the structure of local societies by helping identify or create an appropriate local forum (by which we mean the people, the permission, and the space) for discussing the community's desires.

Funders can provide the resources and time for community members to come together and figure out what matters to them, what they really want for their children and families and neighborhoods, and how those desires translate into aspirations that will guide their work. Note that this work need not entail a whole community visioning process; people can aspire in smaller collaborative groups around specific problems. Funders can then help these groups set priorities for action based on the most urgent concerns or hot-button issues that will engage the community. Funders can enable convening, meeting facilitation, information gathering, and various follow-up tasks. (This might include funding the transportation, child care, and other assistance that will enable community members to attend.) Funders can also help community members learn to communicate their goals and plans in language that will excite and inspire others to get involved.

A program officer at a foundation serving a highly diverse metropolitan area captures our intent in his definition of community building:

> Our working premise has been that community building is, by its very definition, the process through which people come together, cross lines that could divide them, and engage together in the shared experience of identifying issues that are important to them and to the quality of lives in their communities. [They then] make plans together and implement those plans together.

As the aspirations move to action, funders can support the necessary collaboration at a systems level (crossing sector and discipline boundaries) and ensure that grantmaking priorities are flexible enough to respond to community ideas as they are developed. Of course, funders want to see that their contributions are used wisely by the community. This is not just a matter of oversight and auditing, but of funder involvement. Funder involvement of this sort means the funder may play many roles:

- Convener
- Challenger
- Interim fiduciary
- Participant
- Political cover
- Community servant

Funder as convener. Local and national foundations are in a strong position to act as conveners of community work, because, as one program officer admits, "People will return our phone calls." With more modesty, however, he emphasizes that community members "have lots more skills, lots more knowledge, lots more life experience and community experience, and are much more talented than we are." The point is that funders can convene a group of local leaders and residents to develop shared goals and action plans, but they have to recognize that they don't hold all the cards. While funders may bring resources and particular priorities, community members bring most of the experience, local knowledge, and varied perspectives to the work. If funders are going to act as conveners, they need to make explicit to themselves and the community that their interest is in getting to solutions, not in advocating particular positions or preserving particular organizations. Because of perceptions of the power that comes with grantmaking, some communities may be unable to view funders as impartial conveners. In such situations, some other organization in the community may need to be the convener.

Funder as challenger. Depending on the relationship between the funder and the community, some funders can get involved in the process by playing a "challenger" role—gently but firmly continuing to remind the community of the aspirations for which the community is striving and the need for all decisions to be based on reaching these goals. The Annie E. Casey Foundation, a national funder with extensive experience supporting local community collaboration, says, "It helps local participants to have someone in the discussion who is unwavering on the fundamentals; as an 'outsider' this is a lot easier for the foundation to do."[14]

Funder as interim fiduciary. Community work in its early stages usually faces an absence of governance mechanisms and methods of shared financial accountability to facilitate the use of funds across organization boundaries. Also, participants often have insufficient experience addressing conflicts of interest. These characteristics increase the potential for mistakes in early contracting relationships that can adversely affect the entire process. Recognizing this, communities may quickly resort to forming a new nonprofit organization or designating a "lead agency" to fill the fiduciary role. Both of these strategies, as we'll discuss later, may present risks to the process. Another possibility is for the funder to model neutrality and accountability by serving as an interim fiduciary. This gives the community the breathing room to develop its own governance model and financial relationships in accordance with its developing goals and plans.

Funder as participant. Funders, especially at the local level, are already participants in the systems of services that a community uses to address problems. (For example, when a local funder is known for its regular support of research or services on a particular issue or when its staff have become local experts on the issue it supports, the funder is clearly a fellow participant in the community's system.) As such, it is important for community foundations, family foundations, and United Way organizations to participate in the community process to develop high aspirations and the plans for reaching them. In this way, funders can appropriately bring their own agendas to the table to add to the mix of perspectives emerging from all sectors of the community. At the same time, funders can see firsthand how they may need to change their own policies and processes to facilitate progress toward community goals. Instead of waiting in the wings until the community comes with a request, funders can prepare throughout the planning process for how they will apply funding to implementation. National funders should also explore becoming participants in local planning processes in those communities with which they have developed a relationship.

Funder as political cover. Difficult decisions have to be made in the midst of planning and implementing new ways of solving community problems. At times, neighborhood leaders, elected officials, organizational executives, or government administrators may appreciate the ability to shift criticism away from themselves and onto the funder. In other words, they can use the funder as "political cover." When the funder is also a local leader, this may not be in the funder's best interest (because its own need for local appreciation is important), but national funders who are involved in local community planning can usually take on some of this responsibility without a lot of negative repercussions.

Funder as community servant. The previous ways in which a funder can be involved in community work include elements of leadership and control, but funders can also emphasize their servant role. As a community servant, funders behave as good listeners and look for ways to help the community overcome obstacles. They may have a strong role to play in pulling things together, but they emphasize empowering others to succeed and take the credit, not maximizing their own power and glory. The president of one community foundation highlights the servant-leader role of his organization by likening it to the community's central nervous system. Despite all the work that the foundation does to connect people and resources and to support collaboration, he says:

> At the end of the day, the newspaper will write about the donors and the doers, but they're not very interested in the intermediaries that make it all work.... And that's the challenge of being a servant-leader. You're sort of transparent, you're invisible. But behind the scenes, that community nervous system—that's our job.

Encourage broad community engagement

Community engagement is essential for community work. Even a collaborative effort that involves only a few organizations almost always needs buy-in from local residents, donors, and decision makers. And reaching shared aspirations for the community necessarily requires input from and involvement of multiple stakeholders.

Community engagement is an ongoing process of moving out to larger and larger circles of people. A community problem-solving effort may begin with a few individuals or a few organizations, but it needs to continuously seek out additional participants and involve multiple sectors (not just nonprofits, but government agencies, businesses, schools, religious congregations, and others) to be seen and valued as a community-wide effort. As Emil Angelica and Vincent Hyman point out in their book, *Coping with Cutbacks*, increasing the number and variety of participants in a problem-solving effort expands the range of possible solutions. They add, "By increasing engagement with others and letting go of some control of decision making, you [the nonprofit organization] may actually have a better chance of accomplishing your organization's mission, ensuring that its values are furthered, and preserving that which is worthwhile in your organization's programs and services."[15] These benefits would also apply to funders and other community leaders who reach out to ever-wider circles of influence.

Once the core collaborators for any community initiative clarify their shared aspirations, they can begin to involve others who will want to have input into strategies, action steps, resource allocation, and intermediate goals. This work may then engage those who can help with communication, finance, and policy. The more facets of the community that are engaged early in the process, the more likely that community work will experience these benefits:

- Improved understanding of the problem
- Greater awareness of the effort
- Inclusiveness to respond to diverse needs

- Increased support of the effort
- Commitment from those who might otherwise undermine the work

Improved understanding of the problem. Community engagement efforts can include surveys, interviews, and focus groups that uncover how community members feel about a particular issue, what they would like to see done differently, and what they are already doing about it. Such information gathering promotes engagement when multiple stakeholders are directly involved in designing and administering the surveys and analyzing the results.

Greater awareness of the effort. Changing the way work is organized requires consciousness raising; people often need to understand why changes need to be made and how the community will benefit. The more constituencies that are involved in the work of change, the more people will understand the value of it.

Inclusiveness to respond to diverse needs. A truly community-based effort will reflect the diversity within the community while, at the same time, presenting a united commitment to reach shared goals. Most solutions require attention to diversity not only in terms of race and culture, but also in terms of age, faith, socioeconomic status, neighborhood of residence, sector affiliations, and more. Effective community engagement takes advantage of all these multiple viewpoints to enable action that will respond to diverse needs. Efforts to be inclusive can be unsettling. As one program officer says, "Perhaps a good practical test for inclusion is the degree of discomfort caused by the reach." For communities with a history of racism, considerable income disparities, conflicting economic development priorities, and other divisions, a widely diverse community-based effort can be an especially tall order. But it is necessary for success. And we believe it can be facilitated by a focus on high aspirations with which everyone can agree.

Benefits of Broad Community Engagement

- Improved understanding of the problem
- Greater awareness of the effort
- Inclusiveness to respond to diverse needs
- Increased support of the effort
- Commitment from those who might otherwise undermine the work

Increased support of the effort. People are more likely to buy into the goals of the collaborative effort, look for ways to help, and accept the changes that will have to be made in their own work if they have been engaged in the process of information gathering, brainstorming, planning, and action.

Commitment from those who might otherwise undermine the work. Failure to involve important constituents in community change processes can be detrimental, as indicated by this statement from the Annie E. Casey Foundation, "The planning process excluded many who said that because they were left out of key planning decisions, they owed no allegiance to the specific commitments or vision."[16] A lack of allegiance might mean simply ignoring the action of the collaborative, but it could also mean actively trying to undermine its goals. Collaborative groups must engage people of all viewpoints early on and genuinely include them in the process of reaching shared aspirations.

Funders can encourage broad community engagement in a number of ways. These include making announcements throughout the community, making phone calls to ask people to get involved, holding informational meetings, maintaining a database of participants, continually following up on suggestions for who else should be involved, conducting surveys or interviews, and holding large brainstorming sessions.

Funders can also help collaboratives understand that the process of community engagement must be strategic, or well planned, in order to avoid wasting resources, putting people on the spot or on the defensive, or involving constituents too early (so that they drop out before they're most needed). Collaboratives must also understand the need to get all relevant voices to the table (even those who may create tension). One funder talks about "building bridges across boundaries," but emphasizes that funders shouldn't make "bridge building the focus of attention, but rather have the common purpose toward which people are moving be the focus of attention."

The work of the community also moves forward even while the process of engaging more participants continues. Community collaboration cannot be held hostage to those who refuse to become involved, and community groups cannot afford to postpone working toward their aspirations until they're sure that all the right people are coming to every meeting. The point is not to engage all people all the time in all community work, but to ensure that each community planning process will be able to reach its goals by involving all the right people, at the right times, for the right purposes, without leaving out anyone whose perspective or help is essential for success.

Ensure information for community empowerment

Although funders may worry about imposing their own solutions or agendas on the process of community work, communities cannot feel empowered to succeed without access to information. Communities become powerful designers of their own destiny when they have the data and knowledge to make informed decisions.

Nothing is more detrimental to an enthusiastic new community collaborative than to find that the participants' questions about the problem cannot be answered. How often have you attended meetings in which the following conclusions were made, with hands thrown into the air?

- "We can't make a decision until we know the full extent of the problem."
- "We don't know enough about who is affected to know whether we're targeting the right needs."
- "We don't know how much community money we're actually spending on this issue or what services it subsidizes. How do we know what more we need?"
- "We don't know what services have been shown to work."

The usual response is to commission a report, wait six months for the research to be done, and then learn that the data are hard to find or don't reveal the needed information. Plus, by then, the collaborative either has moved on in ways that make the data irrelevant, or has disbanded for lack of direction.

Community Engagement in Action

When Battle Creek, Michigan, began a process in 1999 to track community indicators of its quality of life, the city had a teen pregnancy rate 200 percent higher than the state average and 93 percent higher than the rest of Calhoun County. As a result, community members identified teen pregnancy as a key target area for action.

Ironically, though, when the United Way of Greater Battle Creek solicited grant proposals from local health and human services agencies for programs to reduce the teen pregnancy rate, no proposals were received. This was, unfortunately, consistent with a long history in Battle Creek of failed community efforts on this issue. (Anecdotes from residents discussed attempts going back as far as twenty years.) The issue was seen as "no win" for organizations that depended on the community for funding, because the community was seen as splintered along moral and cultural lines. Community agencies, schools, public health programs, and the justice system were reluctant to become embroiled in community conflict over this issue, and thus were, at best, ineffective in their efforts to prevent teen pregnancy.

The United Way became determined to break this cycle of futility. It quickly enlisted the Battle Creek Community Foundation, W. K. Kellogg Foundation, and Calhoun County Department of Public Health as collaborative partners. This model of "moving out" the ownership of the problem and its solutions to ever-broadening concentric circles was a meaningful shift in approach. Ultimately, the partners hoped that the community as a whole would develop a sense of ownership of this issue, not simply the agencies whose missions should have dictated involvement.

The partners first researched the best practices of successful teen pregnancy prevention efforts in other communities. (A comprehensive report of these research results is available on the Collaboratory web site at www.comnet.org/collaboratorycs/.) The partners learned that, along with multiple strategies, broad community engagement was an element present in all successful programs. In response, they began a process of community convening and shared planning:

- An introductory overview meeting brought together individuals who were concerned about the high teen pregnancy rate. Nearly one hundred people attended the June 2000 meeting. All sectors of the community were represented: schools, nonprofit agencies (from Planned Parenthood to Catholic Social Services), neighborhood centers, criminal justice departments, business and economic development groups, faith-based community organizations, local unions, and involved citizens. A facilitated discussion revealed a shared desire for "our daughters to not become pregnant while they are still children."

- A public relations effort was launched that made extensive use of the local media, billboards, and advertisements to inform the community of the issue and the strategies for solution.

- A widely diverse group of community members drafted a strategic plan for a shared effort to reduce teen pregnancy.

- A second community-wide meeting, held in November 2000, brought together more than seventy-five people to learn about the research and planning and determine the next steps.

- Over a series of meetings in winter and spring 2001, the Teen Pregnancy Prevention Advisory Governing Body was established with the mission to dramatically reduce the rate of teen pregnancy in Calhoun County, Michigan.

- Additional partners were then enlisted, including the University of Michigan, to help the governing body use the Internet and other technologies to keep the community informed, provide information and referral services, provide support to parents, network with other communities and national teen pregnancy organizations, and sustain local community commitment.

While it is too early to measure whether Battle Creek is reducing teen pregnancy, the original partners have succeeded in broadening community engagement and ownership of the process. Their effort has thus resulted in a better understanding of the problem, widespread awareness of ongoing efforts, and a new commitment from diverse players to work together. Most telling is that, in the first United Way funding cycle since the initiation of the community engagement effort, six agencies applied to the United Way for funding of teen pregnancy prevention efforts.

For more information, contact:
Nancy Macfarlane
Director of Community Investments
United Way of Greater Battle Creek
34 West Jackson Street, Suite 4B
Battle Creek, MI 49017
Tel: 616-962-9538
Fax: 616-962-0074
www.uwgbc.org

Community work cannot afford to operate bereft of information. As a senior officer of a national foundation notes:

> We keep hearing over and over two things: … people are not transparent enough about what they're learning, and we're not precise enough about the specifics of what works. Not that anybody wants prescriptions or cookbooks, but people want tools and very specific guidance about what somebody else did and what they ran into so they can build on it.

Funders can play a crucial role in helping communities access information for empowered decision making by

- Supporting the work of quick-turnaround, "lay-of-the-land" research (locally based, nonacademic-style studies to identify promising practices, trends, and community data).

- Encouraging collaborative groups to include representatives from local information resources such as libraries, health departments, chambers of commerce, community colleges and universities, businesses, and service-learning groups.

- Supporting the implementation of management information systems (discussed further below).

- Funding ongoing data collection to track indicators of community progress.

- Connecting collaborative groups to excellent sources for information (including research databases on the web and university-based applied research departments).

Fund Systems

In addition to funding community-wide efforts, funders can support community problem solving by funding work at the level of community systems, instead of at the organizational level. When we talk about "systems," we are referring to all the approaches and actors in a community that are trying to solve a problem. While people often think of "systems" only as government bureaucracies (for example, the public school system, the welfare system), nonprofits and funders are central participants in many other kinds of community systems that are less constrained by definite boundaries and more malleable to action, such as the food assistance system, the arts education system, the youth development system, and the environmental conservation system. Each community has several such systems, involving many different service providers, various public and private funders, diverse clients, locally based businesses, decision makers from boards of trustees and government offices, and others. Work at a systems level crosses sector boundaries, organization divisions, funding streams, and program categories.

Communities today have the leadership and sophistication to become conscious designers of these systems, but they need resources, information, technology, and successful collaboration to reorganize the work. Following are five practical steps that funders can take to fund work at this systems level.

- Make cross-organization grants
- Go beyond nonprofit management support
- Enable multiorganization management information systems
- Support collaborative governance
- Measure systemwide outcomes

Make cross-organization grants

Although the default approach to grantmaking is to write one check to one organization to carry out one program, there is no reason that funding has to be done this way. If funders make grants directly to collaborative groups and multiorganization efforts, they can fund a system of services to solve a problem, rather than separate and uncoordinated activities. Additional benefits include

- No single lead agency
- Resources are pooled
- Economies of scale are produced
- Sustainable investments are enabled

No single lead agency. Often when a neighborhood or community collaborative is formed, grant money is awarded to one of the participants in the collaborative, which is then designated as the lead agency. This agency is expected to manage and allocate the funds, submit reports, and organize the work of the collaborative. While this makes administrative sense and could be perceived as easier for the foundation, having a lead agency can often cause problems for the collaborative. Power dynamics get in the way of working well together, and the lead agency's agenda can begin to take precedence over the community's goals. In addition, the staff and board of the lead agency are often unprepared for the new responsibilities and unable to adequately balance their original role as service provider with their added role as collaborative leader (a role for which they may lack the skills and impartiality).[17] A grant made specifically to a cross-organization project or collaborative, rather than any one organization, avoids these difficulties. (While one organization will have to act as the fiduciary or fiscal agent, this is a separate responsibility from operating as the "lead agency.")

Resources are pooled. Collaboratives are often challenged by the many separate funding streams that flow into a system of services. Any discussion of how to coordinate work across these various sources quickly becomes entangled and seems futile. We will talk more about collaboration among funders to reduce this confusion, but even one funder alone can make a difference by pooling its grants for organizations that operate within the same community system into a collaborative grant for the whole group.

Economies of scale are produced. If you combine several smaller grants into one larger grant for a whole community system, you create the opportunity to purchase technology, supplies, consulting services, and other resources that each organization could never afford by working separately with its smaller piece of the pie. And as collaborative ways of working become the norm, rather than an add-on to daily work, the tools and services that support collaborative work will be increasingly important for organizations to have.

Sustainable investments are enabled. Grantmaking to individual organizations can begin to look like at bats in baseball: If you didn't get a hit the first time up, there's always next time. In their desire to be fair, funders may use this approach. Funding multiple organizations in a collaborative group prevents the need to shift investments from one organization to another each year, while still creating an environment of respect and inclusion for various service providers. As a result, funders can sustain their investment in solutions over many years.

For banking purposes, one organization will have to act as the fiduciary for a grant that is made across organizations (to a collaborative), but this need not (and preferably should not) be one of the participants in the collaborative. It also need not be a brand-new nonprofit organization created just to receive grants for one particular collaborative. Instead, another responsible community agency could be in charge of receiving and distributing the funds, without being the organization that makes the decisions about how the money is used. With the appropriate agreements, the collaborative would still be responsible for maintaining the budget for the funds, making reports to the funder, and being accountable for results. Thus, the power remains with the full collaborative to decide how the funds will best advance the members' shared aspirations.

Go beyond nonprofit management support

"Necessary but not sufficient." This has become our mantra for describing the value of nonprofit management support, a growing field of services and a common strategy used by foundations that are looking to get more impact for their dollars. The prevailing wisdom is that nonprofits fail to achieve solutions and are problematic partners in collaborative efforts because they suffer from inexperienced leadership, unskilled management, and inefficient internal operations. Funders who want to address these deficiencies target some of their donations to workshops, consulting services, and technical assistance that will improve the management capacity of nonprofit organizations.

A Management Information System for the Community

In January 2000, approximately twenty social services agencies in Shreveport, Louisiana, began using a management information system (MIS) called Service Point. Many different types of agencies (both nonprofits and government offices) track multiple populations through Service Point, including people who are homeless or have mental health issues, substance abuse problems, or developmental disabilities.

Service Point is designed to enhance client case management, administration of services, and community-wide planning. The system allows users to track client intake and assessment information, and then track services and referrals provided to clients, their status, and their follow-up needs. It also checks clients in and out of local shelters, tracks the availability of shelter bedspace, provides a searchable directory of agencies and programs in the area, and tracks the amounts and sources of funds used to provide clients with services. Service Point generates standard and customized reports for individual agencies and for the community that can meet the reporting requirements of such federal agencies as HUD and FEMA.

Like all well-designed management information systems, Service Point ensures client confidentiality and security of the information. Users must be authenticated by the system before they gain access to data. In addition, staff can input "restricted" records, meaning that the complete record may only be viewed by the user or agency who entered the information.

Overall administration of Service Point in Shreveport occurs at an information and referral agency called Centerpoint, whose goal is to "serve as a center for managed access to services, the dissemination of information, the compilation of data, and the facilitation of networking for the social services system in the Shreveport-Bossier area." Centerpoint shares responsibility for maintenance of the system with the company that developed it, Bowman Internet Systems. The two organizations share a staff person who is responsible for training, technical support, and report generation.

Individual agencies do not generate their own reports from Service Point. However, community-wide reports are generated and used by the Homeless Coalition of Northwest Louisiana and the Shreveport-Bossier Service Connection, a ninety-member coalition of businesses, governmental and civic leaders, social services providers, and religious organizations.

For more information, contact:
Centerpoint
1002 Texas Avenue
Shreveport, LA 71101
Tel: 318-227-2100
www.centerpt.org

A more extensive description of Service Point and other community homelessness management information systems is available on the Collaboratory's web site at www.comnet.org/collaboratorycs.

While nonprofit management support, or capacity building, is a necessary strategy for improving the capability of the sector, it is not sufficient for enabling community-wide solutions. No matter how much better each organization gets at managing its finances, working with its board, or marketing its services, each nonprofit and each collaborative is still hampered by the sector's and community's fractured approach to problems. Funding for management support for individual organizations is important, but funding for the support of collaborative groups is essential as well. We discuss this further in the next chapter.

Enable multiorganization management information systems

Information technologies are revolutionizing the way work is accomplished today, not only within organizations but also across them. Corporate America is collaborating more than ever because of the information sharing made possible by the world wide web,[18] and we have every reason to expect the nonprofit and public sectors to do the same. The Internet, collaborative technologies, and management information systems make it possible for communities to take social issues consigned to the "soft" sciences and work on them with "hard" solutions based on data rather than hunches or anecdotal evidence.

Multiorganization management information systems (MISs) directly benefit clients by enabling collaborative case management: Information about a client's history and progress is seen and updated by case workers in different organizations so that a comprehensive plan of services can address the client's needs, which are usually complex. In addition, management information systems make it possible for the community to understand and improve its whole system of services. Communities that have implemented a multiorganization management information system to improve their services find that the system

- Provides an accurate and easily updated community-wide picture of how many people are using what kinds of services with what results.

- Provides an accurate and easily updated community-wide picture of how much money is being spent on services and for what results (what some people have termed "the return on social investment"). This can enable more appropriate resource allocation in the community and more efficient use of funds.

- Allows the community to be more responsive to demands of public and private funders for more accurate and consistent reporting of outcomes and use of funds.

- Builds the capacity of agencies and the community to know what they need to do and what resources it takes to do it, and to use data to make a convincing case to funders.

- Reveals and prevents duplication of services while highlighting gaps in services.

- Allows service providers to work together more as a community by enhancing communication across agencies (and, thus, diminishing turf battles and distrust).[19]

In addition to these benefits, the purchase and administration of one management information system for a whole system of services is dramatically cheaper for funders and the community than for each organization to operate its own system or to try to connect several unique systems into a community-wide data warehouse. Many well-tested management information systems have already been designed to help communities meet these goals and ensure confidentiality of data as necessary. The challenge now is to ensure that each organization in the system has the appropriate hardware and technical assistance and that the community is supported in the process of adopting, adapting, negotiating ownership of, implementing, and maintaining these collaborative technologies.

Support collaborative governance

The Center for the Study of Social Policy states that "local governance entities can be the place where a group of citizens considers how to marshal all parts of the community … to a common aim."[20] Such collaborative governance is necessary for systems change, because decisions have to be made in a shared space—the uncharted territory located between organization boundaries and traditional leadership hierarchies. Communities need to create and make better use of governance bodies that are expected to

- Engage the community—By moving out to broader and broader circles of engagement, collaborative governance bodies act as ambassadors *from* the community, representing the concerns of residents, local leaders, nonprofits, government, and others.

- Understand and improve the system of services—These bodies explore who does what, how resources are used, what results are obtained, how multiple strategies can be preserved as needed, and what is required to improve the community's efforts to systemically solve problems. They are then charged with overseeing the implementation of changes and may allocate resources to improve the system.

- Evaluate efforts—A collaborative governance structure stays focused on desired results and regularly evaluates progress toward the community's goals. It holds itself and the system accountable for reaching solutions.

- Ensure sustainability—Improvements at a systems level are easily derailed by the complexity of the effort, turnover of staff, new regulations, changes in funding, and so on. A governance body creates a permanent structure that maintains attention to the tasks that need to be done, the results of implementation, ongoing refinement of plans, and, ultimately, the shift to prevention of problems.

Governance bodies are usually made up of volunteers who participate in the governance task as concerned citizens or as representatives from their professions or organizations. Initiators of a governance body must address many issues that can affect the community's perception of the body, its neutrality, and its ability to succeed, including: who creates the body, how members are chosen, who participates, where they meet, who facilitates meetings, how much control they have to make decisions, and so on.

Community Governance in Action

The Local Investment Commission (LINC) is a thirty-six-member citizen governing board focused on improving the lives of children and families in Kansas City and Jackson County, Missouri.[21] The members are volunteers from the business and neighborhood leadership of the community, but they represent the community, not their own businesses or organizations; the commission does not include providers or elected officials. Additional volunteers serve on standing and working committees, making up a community collaborative of over seven hundred residents. A nonvoting "professional cabinet" of nonprofit and government agency service providers are asked to share their perspectives with the commission, and a full-time staff provide administrative and research support. Initial and ongoing funding for LINC has come from the Missouri Caring Communities Fund, which was created through a collaboration of seven state departments—Social Services, Mental Health, Health, Labor, Education, Corrections, and Economic Development—to enable school-linked, neighborhood-based services. Other grants have supported LINC's involvement in welfare-to-work, after-school care, new business development in the central city, and health care.

LINC's mission is "to provide leadership and influence to engage the Kansas City community in creating the best system to support and strengthen children, families, and individuals, holding that system accountable, and changing public attitudes toward the system." Since its inception in 1992, LINC has helped the community improve a variety of services and their outcomes. For example, its welfare-to-work efforts have filled 6,100 area jobs since 1995, and over 4,000 former welfare recipients are still employed. In addition, LINC rescued the community's before- and after-school child care program just before it was discontinued because of lack of funds; since then, over 6,800 students have enrolled in such programs at eighteen schools.

LINC also helped decentralize the local Department of Family Services and relocate staff to neighborhood offices, and it has established over forty-five school-based social services centers for children and families.

For more information, contact:
Local Investment Commission
3100 Broadway, Suite 226
Kansas City, MO 64111
Tel: 816-889-5050, Fax: 816-889-5051
www.kclinc.org

The Appendix, Community Governance Strategies, on pages 94–95, describes options for structuring a community governance entity.

Funders can support collaborative governance by seeing that these up-front issues are carefully addressed and that the body has behind-the-scenes support to do its work. This can be done through funding excellent consulting services or a local organization whose purpose is to support community collaboration. (Funding support services to sustain community problem solving is discussed in Chapter Three.)

Measure systemwide outcomes

As funders begin to support strategies for communities to work across organizations and at a systems level, evaluation will have to look at improvements at a systems level. No longer does it make sense to hold individual organizations accountable for social problem solving when the solutions can only be obtained through cross-organization efforts. Therefore, calls for accountability, reporting requirements, and funding for evaluation must now be designed to capture improvements in the system of services and the lives of people served by the whole system. A management information system is essential to this task, because data will have to be collected from multiple programs, organizations, clients, and funding streams to answer the question, How are we doing? Today's advances in technology allow communities to engage in systemic changes that previously seemed impossible.

While funders have already supported efforts to measure outcomes within individual organizations and to develop a set of indicators to use in tracking community improvement, the essential next step toward better evaluation is to support the examination of systemwide outcomes.[22] Not only will this give communities a better sense of where they are and where they're going, but also attention to these outcomes will encourage broader participation in community problem solving by highlighting results that matter to most residents (such as more people being employed) rather than outcomes that don't address their concerns (such as

Calls for accountability, reporting requirements, and funding for evaluation must be designed to capture improvements in the system of services and the lives of people served by the whole system.

how many workshop participants said that their attitude had changed about the value of work).

Be the Change You Wish to See

In order to fund communities and systems, funders will have to rethink their internal processes. As Mahatma Gandhi said, "Be the change you wish to see in the world." We believe that if funders want positive impact, they will have to demonstrate their commitment to coordinated strategies and systemic solutions by incorporating the following new ways of working into their own daily activities:

- Structure the giving process to fund communities and systems
- Call grantees to their highest aspirations
- Prepare foundation board members to be change agents
- Collaborate with other funders
- Support an infrastructure

Structure the giving process to fund communities and systems

Most foundations have an organization chart designed around fragmented approaches to social issues. However, separate giving areas with separate program officers may discourage solution-centered, systemic community work. When a funder structures its own work in a comprehensive manner, like the work it would like to see in communities, it will grasp the implications of its requirements. It will also understand the opportunities it has to model and encourage community problem solving.

The Northwest Area Foundation recently took this realization to heart when it replaced its practice of short-term grants to hundreds of nonprofit organizations with a limited number of ten-year, multimillion dollar partnerships with whole communities. Each partnership emphasizes a strategic approach to reducing poverty. An article in the *Chronicle of Philanthropy* notes that the foundation "opted for a pioneering course of working not just through nonprofit groups but directly with entire communities," and included businesses, churches, schools, and local governments in the partnerships. While it's too soon to measure results, the foundation believes that funding community-wide partnerships has to be a better way to make a difference than project-by-project grantmaking.[23]

Funders that are looking to fund communities and systems would do well to consider their entire process—from requests for proposals to evaluation—as open to reengineering. This would mirror the process that should occur in communities. Funders might do the following:

- Focus on a whole community system, such as early childhood care, that is of concern to communities supported by the funder.

- Identify all the issues, roles, players, and services that are swirling around within that system.

- Organize foundation staff to represent each major aspect of the system, but ensure that all decisions are made as a group.

- Ask communities to clarify their highest aspirations for this system, which can then affirm the foundation's highest aspirations as well.

- Make grants to a community's collaborative governing body for that system, and expect unlikely partners to be invited (for example, hospitals getting involved with transportation issues, or chambers of commerce helping with affordable housing).

- Make grants to individual organizations whose requests grow out of participation in systemwide problem-solving efforts and are supported by the larger group.

- Ensure that significant and sustained funding is targeted toward the support services and technology needed for community collaboration, not just for direct services within the system.

- Look for, require, and enable systemwide outcomes measurement rather than organization or program outcomes.

- Ensure that the foundation's internal processes and controls model the efficiency and financial accountability expected of high-performing communities (for example, how streamlined is the grant approval process, how quickly is grant money sent, how up-to-date are the funder's management information systems?).

While these new giving strategies may disrupt old patterns of giving in the short term, such a solutions-based structure within the funding organization moves funders from episodic interventions to sustained investments. When the focus is on disparate programs, funders worry about fairness and spreading the giving around. When the focus is on systems and communities, funders can explain their giving decisions on the basis of problem solving, sustainability, cohesiveness, and efficiency. Not only are the new giving strategies better for grantees and the community, but also they can directly benefit funders (such as community foundations) who depend on continued donations for their own work. That is to say, donors are more likely to contribute to foundations that are successful in enabling community problem solving.

Call grantees to their highest aspirations

Setting goals and coming to consensus are not two sides of the same coin. Consensus is the point at which community members can agree, but this point of agreement may not be the most worthy or inspiring goal. The "least common denominator" is certainly not the point of aspiration. Funders need to focus their resources on the highest aspirations for the communities they serve. They are not in the political business of consensus; in fact, they are granted a unique role in society to call for something beyond the kind of "negotiated" vision that falls short of what people really want. While setting high aspirations may also require community members to "agree to disagree" about strategies, it creates the space for multiple, varied approaches to success.

For example, the Kahanoff Foundation in Calgary, Alberta, Canada, challenged its community to greater aspirations in response to an increasing need for nonprofit office space. Individual organizations were approaching the foundation for assistance in finding space in a tight and high-priced office rental market. The community consensus was that nonprofits needed help finding affordable work space. But instead of piecemeal efforts to "save" nonprofits when their leases ran out or rents were raised, the foundation pushed for a broader community response. Foundation leaders met with business and nonprofit leaders to ask, What's the opportunity here? The foundation wondered what the nonprofits could achieve if they were not distracted by the possibility of losing space. During a year of discussions, it determined that providing shared space for multiple nonprofits could be a catalyst for systemic solutions for their community, allowing unprecedented partnerships and better use of resources. Thus, the foundation pushed community members to think bigger and aspire higher. In July 2001, a ten-story office building became the first structure in what is being envisioned as Calgary's nonprofit community campus.

When funders make grants, they cannot allow the initiatives to fail merely for lack of inspiration. The work of assembling, aligning, and developing the resources for shared community work is intensive. If the envisioned outcome doesn't rise to an aspiration, members of the community easily drift away in a fog of So what? On the other hand, the gravitational pull of a community's aspirations will bring engagement and energy to the group work. We recommend that all grant requests and reports from funded projects require grantees to articulate their highest aspirations for the initiative and the community and demonstrate how all project tasks emerge from and contribute to reaching these aspirations.

> **If the envisioned outcome doesn't rise to an aspiration, members of the community easily drift away in a fog of So what? On the other hand, the gravitational pull of a community's aspirations will bring engagement and energy to the group work.**

Prepare foundation board members to be change agents

Reengineering a funder's internal processes will intimately involve its board members, not only in envisioning and sanctioning the changes, but also in defending their decisions to multiple constituents. Any effort to fundamentally change how allocations are made or how progress is assessed in a community must be mindful of the fact that board members are the ones most exposed to the slings and arrows of outraged beneficiaries. Board members may also be vulnerable to criticism from peers in the local community or wider society who feel that their own charitable "favorites" are threatened. Leaders of local community foundations and United Ways are particularly susceptible to these judgments.

Foundation board members must not be expected to defend what they haven't embraced. Instead, their staff must prepare them to be change agents. Board members need to be brought through the process of understanding and owning why this shift in giving is taking place—why the environment makes it possible and necessary, why traditional forms of grantmaking are less effective in helping communities and people, why the desire to solve problems requires systemic approaches, why these new approaches will require new skills and support services. Board meetings about these changes could include role-play exercises to help board members explain the new approaches, discussions of suggested responses and sound bites, and regular exploration of how grantmaking is fitting with community aspirations and the foundation's new structure.

Provide Foundation Board Members with the Knowledge to Be Change Agents

Help board members understand why:

- The environment makes it possible and necessary to change funding approaches
- Traditional forms of grantmaking are failing to help communities
- Solving community problems requires systemic approaches
- New approaches will require new skills and support services

Collaborate with other funders

While restructuring internal foundation processes to support communities and systems is a significant challenge, funders who begin this work will quickly realize that they cannot go on operating in isolation from each other. The work of solving problems through community collaboration and systems reform is simply too big for one funder to do alone, and the need for coordinated resources for community success requires multiple funders to buy into the process and complement one another's grantmaking. Funder collaboration is needed at both the local level, within communities, and at the national level, across communities. Although collaborating with other funders can be challenging, the potential benefits to the funders and the community are many.

1. A funder collaborative can reach for broader community outcomes, envisioning and facilitating solutions that improve the quality of life for the whole community, rather than settling for the results of discrete programs and services. As a consequence, participating foundations experience the pleasure of seeing their resources tackle complex problems with greater success. Likewise, funder collaboratives become a catalyst for increased community involvement in problem solving as diverse stakeholders come together to make the most of pooled resources.

2. Foundations that have long encouraged or required collaboration among their grantees can now demonstrate their commitment to this approach by undertaking the effort themselves. In this way, foundations learn firsthand what it takes to collaborate successfully, and grantees gain a stronger sense of partnership with their funders.

3. If planned in advance, financial accounting and outcomes tracking can be streamlined for both foundations and agencies. Many separate grants with various and sometimes conflicting procedural and reporting requirements can be replaced by one set of expectations from all funders to all grantees. Not only could this improve efficiency on both sides, and enable multiorganization grants, but also it would allow funders and the community to make sense of the costs and benefits of addressing whole problems—information essential for community-wide planning.

4. When funders come together with a shared vision and pooled resources, they have greater leverage to advocate for public policy reform that will align and coordinate government resources on behalf of community problem solving.

5. Funder collaboratives create a valuable forum for foundation leaders to put their heads together. As simple as this may sound, breakthrough ideas and meaningful visions can result when funders regularly interact around significant problems and share their varied expertise and broad perspectives on community life.

Suggestions for creating and operating an effective funder collaboration include the following:

- Involve diverse funders who can bring expertise on issues or valuable connections.

- Seek membership from national foundations in local collaboratives.

- Give each funder one vote in collaborative decisions regardless of the level of financial contribution.

- Establish a shared understanding of what the funder collaborative will accomplish, and then design the collaborative structure to meet those goals. (How often will you meet, for what purposes, for what results?)

- Develop and work toward short-term goals, but prepare for long-term engagement.

- Distinguish between the purpose of pooled resources and the continuing role of individual grantors. (While the collaborative will want to encourage many funders to get involved, it also does not want to deter funders from continuing their own initiatives as well.)

- Explore the possibility of combining the power of private and public funds.

- Decide early on how logistical and administrative tasks will be handled.[24]

Funder Collaboration in Action

Perhaps nothing signifies the breakdown of community more vividly than people rioting in the streets—setting fires, destroying property, unleashing rage and frustration on anyone and anything within reach. Whatever factors get a community to such a breaking point have to be addressed when rebuilding that community. A group of local and national foundations realized the enormity of such a task when considering how to respond to the 1992 Los Angeles riots that brought widespread attention to the city's neglected neighborhoods and residents. In order to maximize their resources and knowledge to address complex needs, they created an alliance, known as Los Angeles Urban Funders (LAUF), to pool funds and share responsibility for empowering low-income neighborhoods to renew their sense of community.[25]

LAUF was housed within the Southern California Association for Philanthropy (SCAP). In 1995, LAUF established its own board of directors with seven foundations. By 2000, thirty family, corporate, and community foundations were participating in LAUF, with each funder receiving one vote on the board. Members include the James Irvine Foundation, BankAmerica Foundation, Fannie Mae Foundation, L.A. United Methodist Urban Foundation, Boeing Employees Community Fund, and California Community Foundation.

LAUF hired two full-time staff members who coordinate five-year comprehensive initiatives in three Los Angeles neighborhoods. Pooled funds provide up to $1 million for each neighborhood. The purpose of the funds is to help neighborhoods develop the partnerships, leadership, data, and strategies necessary to implement improvements. LAUF members participate in neighborhood visioning processes to clarify their own roles in creating change. Funding for specific projects and agencies is still provided through grants from individual grantmakers, whether or not they are part of LAUF. "We want to catalyze and enhance the effectiveness of all grants," says Elwood Hopkins, LAUF's project director.

LAUF has succeeded in helping one neighborhood design a streamlined system for job placement and in helping another neighborhood develop a set of community standards that improved the availability of fresh food. LAUF has enhanced the work of its member funders by providing a better understanding of the neighborhood contexts in which their grantmaking takes place and allowing funders to bring nonfinancial resources, including access to policy makers, to these neighborhoods.

For more information, contact:
Los Angeles Urban Funders
c/o Southern California Association for Philanthropy
315 West 9th Street
Los Angeles, CA 90015
Tel: 213-627-6387
Fax: 213-489-7320
www.scap.org

Support an infrastructure

If funders begin to require more from communities and themselves in terms of high aspirations, broad engagement in collaborative problem solving, and systemwide outcomes, then one more challenge to communities and foundations presents itself: Who is going to do all the work? There is much more to these ideas than grantmaking or coming to meetings. While shifting funding priorities and processes is part of the effort, someone will also have to take up the responsibilities of involving more and more people in the work, facilitating community groups, researching relevant data, administering multiorganization grants, measuring systemwide outcomes, gathering resident feedback, implementing management information systems, handling the logistics of funder collaboratives, and so on.

While staff at large funding organizations may be able to take on some of this work, and volunteers from each collaborative group may be willing to do some of it, these arrangements are usually temporary solutions. Collaborative groups may then turn to the "501(c)(3) solution," which declares, "We'll turn our collaborative group into its own legal entity so we can apply for grants and hire staff." This *sounds* attractive, but it is costly and time consuming and creates a permanent structure that has to be "fed and kept alive" regardless of the life cycle of the collaboration or progress toward its aspirations.

Even so, community problem solving requires some kind of supportive infrastructure to accomplish the multiple tasks of collaborative work and ensure that the process doesn't get stuck. The following chapter discusses various support services for community efforts and a special infrastructure that could bring these services together on behalf of multiple collaborative efforts in the community.

How to Support and Sustain Community Problem Solving

FOR MANY COMMUNITIES, THE PROBLEM-SOLVING APPROACHES described thus far are under way in some form—diverse groups are engaged in shared processes, efforts are being coordinated across systems, management information technology is being implemented. But these changes are hard going, and desired results can be elusive. For long-term success, community work must be sustained past the inevitable hurdles, slow periods, and changes in leadership.

People tend to think that organization leaders or service providers are the ones responsible for sustaining a social-change collaborative. You can see from other professions, however, that the most visible group of workers doesn't accomplish a goal on its own: A team of ballplayers isn't expected to win a championship without coaches, athletic trainers, doctors, and physical therapists. A cast of actors isn't expected to make a movie without cinematographers, designers, acting coaches, editors, and technicians. A crew of carpenters, bricklayers, and electricians isn't expected to build a building without site managers and designers.

In most parts of society, whenever a diverse group of people wants to accomplish something, they need support from other people to get the job done. Not just leadership (the head coach, the director, or the manager), but behind-the-scenes specialists and organizers who serve the needs of the group. Nobody thinks the actors, athletes, or carpenters are "disempowered" because others help them. However, when communities collaborate, people seem to forget that group work requires support.

When funders decide to foster successful community problem solving, they would do well to invest also in the behind-the-scenes specialists, organizers, and coaches that are necessary to sustain the effort and get results. Planning together, implementing shared approaches, and sustaining action require support. Collaborative efforts need someone who maintains progress between meetings and in the face of participant turnover. They need someone who is keeping an eye on the ball at all times—finding answers to questions, involving additional participants as necessary, handling logistical details, and assuring that the process is achieving results. They also need someone who will continually remind the group of its highest aspirations and challenge attempts at compromise or consensus that fall short of these aspirations.

After ten years of providing support services to community problem solving in a large, diverse community, one local funder (quoted earlier) observes, "You need to fund full-time glue and connective tissue in community work." He believes it is essential to have staff supporting broad-based community partnerships, because "you're trying to build a central nervous system for your community, to create another way information is passed around the community and received and processed and utilized. And this just takes full-time work."

Otis Johnson, director of the Savannah Youth Futures Authority (a comprehensive systems reform effort), says that three kinds of support are needed to change the way an entire community assists needy families and children: (1) someone who manages the data and keeps meticulous track of the results; (2) someone who functions as a networker to keep the politics and the communications among agencies running smoothly; and (3) someone who looks at the big picture and pays attention to long-term goals and planning.[26]

The Aspen Institute's study of comprehensive community initiatives reveals the need for core staff who "facilitate the planning process and take responsibility for moving from planning to action" and for technical assistance to help community participants understand particular social issues or funding streams. Aspen Institute recommends a coach who can be objective and provide advice and guidance to the various participants in an initiative.[27]

Charles Bruner, a former Iowa state senator now with the Child and Family Policy Center, writes about this need for support as a major finding of his research on comprehensive community reforms:

> This [community work] requires a form of support and technical assistance that is flexible, individualized, comprehensive, community-based, asset-oriented, seamless, and timely. It requires intensity and duration of involvement, a long-term commitment that most national technical assistance providers do not now provide. It requires a much better coordination of the technical assistance that is offered, avoiding mixed messages that can overwhelm sites receiving advice from all directions.[28]

One foundation program officer we interviewed emphasizes the need for a "community educator" or "community facilitator" who can work behind the scenes to encourage basic community organizing, enable nonconfrontational community problem solving, negotiate relationships among people, keep the lines of communication open, and secure the financial and technological resources needed to pursue community plans. He observes, "A key ingredient for this comprehensive community building work that I have come to believe ... is indispensable is that of [community] educator." In describing a similar role, a community foundation leader talked about a convener that has a "certain nimbleness" and "entrepreneurial spirit," that understands each sector's point of view, and that can speak in the language of each sector.

A senior associate with a national foundation also recognizes that such community-wide assistance is necessary:

> Having a locally based resource and a locally based support system is really important.... If a community is going to solve problems in an ongoing way, it needs ways to access models and approaches and good ideas and people and so forth. Having a local resource that can do that on behalf of groups around the community makes a whole lot of sense.

Funders interested in community-wide solutions must plan how to undergird community work with an infrastructure of support services. If collaboration is an essential strategy for community problem solving, then funders and community leaders must become aggressively intentional about their commitment to behind-the-scenes support.

The remainder of this chapter looks at many opportunities to use supportive services. As Figure 2, Support Services for Community Problem Solving, shows, funders and communities can move along several spectrums as they evolve their plans for sustaining problem-solving efforts. They can choose from a variety of duties for their support specialists, from something as simple as handling the logistical details of meetings to something more complex such as connecting collaborative groups with policy makers. They can also choose different strategies for how to provide this support, from asking a volunteer in a collaborative group to instituting a community-wide infrastructure of support services for multiple collaborative efforts. Finally, they can hold these support specialists to certain criteria of excellence, asking for increasingly sophisticated support as the community's needs become more complicated.

Funders may find it helpful to use these spectrums to assess current support services in the communities with which they work. They may also be able to adapt the choices to how they think about funding community work (see Chapter Four for more about funder self-assessment). The following pages explore these spectrums in more detail as we discuss how a community can meet its needs for support to sustain problem-solving efforts.

Figure 2. Support Services for Community Problem Solving

Support Opportunities Spectrum

A continuum of choices for the kinds of support that can assist community efforts to solve problems, from simple to more complex.

Logistics (convening meetings, and so forth)	Getting people involved	Research (gathering data and case studies to inform decisions)	Information management (keeping information flowing, collecting new data)	Connecting multiple collaborations	Bridging community work with policy making	Tracking outcomes and returns on investments	Serving multiple collaboratives through one community support organization

Support Specialists Spectrum

A continuum of choices for who can provide support services for community problem solving, from an individual serving one group to an infrastructure capable of serving multiple collaborations.

Volunteer participant in the collaborative group	Paid participant in the collaborative group	Paid assistant hired by collaborative group	Staff of a local foundation, United Way, or other community organization	Staff of a community support organization specifically designed to serve multiple collaborative efforts

Support Characteristics Spectrum

A continuum of descriptive characteristics of support specialists. As a community moves forward on the other spectrums, the environment for support becomes increasingly complex, requiring support specialists to become more sophisticated in working with varied perspectives and negotiating progress across dimensions.

Servant-leaders	Neutral players	Seasoned professionals with technical expertise	Bridge builders across sectors

Characteristics of Support

Every community needs individuals who have the skills, time, and commitment to do the between-meeting tasks that allow community work to progress. This provides a stability that is essential for collaborative efforts built around the volunteer time of community leaders and the ever-changing faces of government officials and nonprofit executives. Like the manager at a construction site who attends to the whole building while carpenters, plumbers, and electricians come and go, the support staff keep the collaborative process moving along, even as the participants may change.

What these support specialists do, and how they are defined, depends on how much the community is trying to work at a systems level (across all sectors) to address social challenges. The more engaged the community, the more connected the various efforts, the more complex the support needed to undergird the community's work. In our experience working with communities, we find that as the complexity of the work increases, the type of support specialists required changes.

Like the manager at a construction site who attends to the whole building while carpenters, plumbers, and electricians come and go, the support staff keep the collaborative process moving along, even as the participants may change.

First, we believe that whoever provides such behind-the-scenes services will be most effective in a position of *servant-leader*.[29] While the focus of support specialists is on service—providing whatever the collaborative group needs to succeed—they are also allied visionaries committed to the high aspirations of the group and capable of providing guidance and inspiration when necessary.

Second, we have also seen that communities quickly learn the value of servant-leaders who are *neutral players*—support specialists who are not already aligned with one agenda or solution. By committing themselves to the success of alliances—over and above the success of any participating organization, program, or project—neutral players remain impartial in their relation to any one leader, organization, or sector. In keeping with this neutral position, they should not be direct service providers or run their own community programs. The participants in the collaboratives need to know that the support specialists have the best interests of the group in mind and are only working to enable the community to reach its aspirations.

In addition, although we talk about these servant-leaders as support staff, their responsibilities are often broad and demanding. The kind of support that our research has shown to be essential to sustaining community groups cannot be simply assigned as additional duties to someone's administrative assistant. Much of this support requires the skill of a seasoned professional who understands how to motivate people and navigate difficult terrain. As community-wide problem solving becomes more complex, support specialists will need to provide expertise on knowledge management, information technology, report writing, and outcomes measurement.

Finally, we have found that those organizations and individuals who are supporting complex community-wide efforts soon become champions for community improvement across all sectors, and effective bridge builders to policy makers, opinion leaders, funders, and other communities. Recognizing the complexity of changing large systems, they broaden the circles of engagement farther and farther.

Practical Support Services

What are the tasks of support specialists? We will discuss a variety of options throughout the rest of this chapter. Here are some of the more practical services that support specialists may provide.

- Getting people to participate
- Basing work on shared aspirations
- Making meetings happen
- Making meetings matter
- Following up between meetings
- Managing information

Getting people to participate

To get the broad community engagement necessary for systemic solutions, support specialists for community problem solving spend a lot of time encouraging individuals to join particular collaborative groups. They develop an ever-growing list of potential participants and have many one-on-one conversations to explain the goals of the collaboration, past work, and the importance of participation. They follow up these conversations with information packets and, once the individual has become involved, regularly express appreciation for his or her commitment. This ongoing process helps each collaboration involve an ever-wider circle of influencers, from policy makers, to business executives, to neighborhood leaders, to funders. And it ensures an orientation for each new participant so that the rest of the collaborative members are not continually backtracking to bring new people up to speed.

Basing work on shared aspirations

One of the first responsibilities of the support specialist is to ensure that the group knows its purpose and bases all of its decisions and actions on reaching its shared goal for the community. (The support specialist can post this goal on the wall at every meeting and highlight it in reports and announcements.)

Making meetings happen

Support providers for collaborative groups also make sure the basic administrative tasks of group work are handled efficiently. They should develop a schedule of meetings so that participants know far in advance when meetings will occur. They then locate meeting space, send out meeting notices and directions to the location, and mail any preparatory materials in a timely fashion, including the meeting agenda.

Making meetings matter

Support specialists make each meeting worth the participants' time. In consultation with members of the collaborative, they prepare meaningful and interesting agendas and adequate background information. They ensure that presentations are organized and clear and will keep people's attention. They may also help presenters prepare materials and practice their presentation. In addition, support specialists may brief the chairperson ahead of time so that the meeting runs smoothly.

Support specialists should attend the meetings and help keep the conversation focused on the goals of the collaboration, while guaranteeing that other issues are noted and tracked for future discussion. Through facilitation at meetings and conversations between meetings, they challenge participants to be guided by their highest aspirations for their community so that decisions do not devolve into lowest-common-denominator compromises. Each meeting is evaluated by all participants for its content, structure, pace, and progress toward goals.

Following up between meetings

While participants in collaborative groups often leave the meeting to return to a mountain of other responsibilities, support specialists should keep the collaboration foremost in their daily work. Minutes from the meeting and a summary of the evaluations are prepared as quickly as possible and sent to all interested parties. If research needs to be done about an issue raised in the meeting or promising practices from other communities, support specialists start studying the matter in the hopes of finding an answer before the next meeting. Summary reports are then sent in advance of the meeting, with suggestions for how participants can use the information. If guests need to be invited to the next meeting, or additional new participants need to be recruited, staff have the responsibility to make these calls.

Support specialists are also available between meetings to coach participants in the problem-solving and group-process skills needed for effective collaborative work. Thus, the support staff for collaborative groups should excel in group facilitation, including being able to promote meaningful dialogue, provide positive engagement, and give constructive feedback. Because of their neutrality, they can use these skills effectively in the community.

(Of course, community members also need to use these skills in their collaborative work, but they may need help in developing and practicing them. While participants can receive group dynamics training at one or more of their meetings, they sometimes need private mentoring in how to handle an emergency conflict, how to see an issue from someone else's point of view, and how to listen. These conversations are also a welcome opportunity for support staff to remind participants of the purpose and aspirations of the collaboration.)

Managing information

Much of the rest of a support specialist's responsibilities fall into the broad category of information management—organizing, tracking, and communicating various kinds of information. With the right support, collaboratives can take advantage of advances in technology that enable information to be managed as never before.

In addition to communication about and between meetings, other examples of information management include

- Keeping databases of participants in collaborations.
- Keeping databases of local services to clarify the structure of community systems.
- Hosting a management information system used by multiple service providers to track data about clients and services provided; such a management information system enables better case management for integrated services and better community-wide data collection for policy and funding decisions.
- Managing funding information by tracking grant opportunities, administering grants for collaboratives, and providing services to a local funder collaborative.

- Helping participants in collaborative groups use various collaborative technologies (listservs, document sharing, application service providers, and so forth) to keep information flowing across organization and sector boundaries.

Tapping the Full Potential of a Supportive Infrastructure

Communities that have found a way to sustain their collaborative work through dedicated support specialists have come to rely on this infrastructure as a key resource for positive change. Collaborative groups turn to such servant-leaders not only for the practical support that allows group work to thrive, but also for the assistance that keeps the larger community on track toward systemwide solutions. Support specialists are often well positioned to make the case for coordinated approaches, create the political resolve to effect change, remove barriers to implementation, build relationships across traditional boundaries, and prevent conflicts while not allowing the community to take no for an answer. They can challenge community leaders to reach for the highest aspirations for their residents, and then keep community work from getting stuck in the process of turning visions into action. They can also help the community respond to increasing government mandates for community-based collaboratives and governing bodies.

To realize even greater potential for support services—and enhance their sustainability—a community can put together an infrastructure to serve multiple coalitions and collaborative groups while providing a link among these integrated efforts. This can spread the cost of supporting multiple collaborative efforts while preventing the community from having to create a whole slew of new 501(c)(3) organizations for all their collaborative groups. And, as the support needs of each collaborative group ebb and flow over time, the support services can be targeted appropriately, allowing people and funding to be applied in a just-in-time fashion.

When support specialists assist more than one collaborative effort, they become uniquely charged with working in the space shared by nonprofit, government, and business sectors of the community. This positions them to keep their finger on the pulse of all community-level work. By knowing which people are involved in which collaboratives with which goals, they can see and inform the community when activities are beginning to overlap, how decisions on one issue will impact another, when policy reform is going to be needed, and how funding can be reorganized to better serve the community. Also, as processes or data are learned through the work of one collaborative, the support staff can share this with another collaborative that will benefit from the same knowledge.

Support Services in Action:
Finding Unspent Resources and Getting Children What They Deserve

The Northern California Council for the Community (NCCC) acts as a supportive entity for community problem solving in the San Francisco Bay area.[30] NCCC has convened a broad-based coalition of community leaders called the Bay Area Partnership. Membership includes representatives from the regional offices of five federal departments, ten county governments, two United Ways, and numerous community-based philanthropic organizations. Members are united by a common commitment to obtain better outcomes for children and families through more integrated, collaborative neighborhood- and community-based approaches.

NCCC serves as "secretariat," which involves doing administrative tasks (keeping the database of members, sending out announcements, developing meeting agendas, producing minutes), providing research data to inform the partnership's ideas for change, and receiving grant funds on behalf of the partnership.

NCCC staff used mapping and census data to help the partnership identify fifty-two neighborhoods in which a major portion of the Bay Area's impoverished families live so that systemic efforts to improve lives could be targeted to those neighborhoods most in need. One of the first projects they undertook was to improve children's access to in-school nutrition and extended-day programs. Ed Schoenberger, NCCC's president, explained the task this way:

The presence of a supportive infrastructure in the community, serving and connecting multiple collaborative efforts, makes possible many of the suggestions made in the previous chapter:

- By encouraging community engagement in the full system of social problem solving, the supportive infrastructure enables a focus on "What do we want?" and on community-wide or systemwide outcomes rather than individual agency outcomes.

- By actively involving a wide range of stakeholders in any collaborative effort, the supportive infrastructure enables and undergirds the work of collaborative governance.

- By bringing a problem-solving bias to the goal of improving efficiency (not just mergers to reduce duplication), the infrastructure helps the

"We discovered that there was a lot of federal and state money for nutrition programs that wasn't being spent. And a lot of the school districts serving those neighborhoods weren't applying for that money. With the help of key federal administrators, children and youth advocates, and educational leaders, we actually published a list of school districts, citing those numbers, those neighborhoods, and then all of the sudden everybody got excited, and said, 'You're serving a neighborhood where there's 70 percent or 60 percent low-income kids, and you're not offering snack programs, you're not offering breakfast programs?' Phones just started jumping off the hook. And in the following year and a half or so, there were about fifty or sixty new programs in Bay Area schools, serving those neighborhoods."

The partnership, he concluded, "Provided the forum by which the right people were in the right room at the same time to say, 'You know, we could do something about this if we really wanted to.'" As the behind-the-scenes support, NCCC brought these people together and then provided the background research and the information dissemination to help the partnership realize its goal. Buoyed by its success, the partnership is now tackling a broad range of issues around workforce development, child development, and related issues affecting the fifty-two neighborhoods.

For more information, contact:
Northern California Council for the Community
50 California Street, Suite 450
San Francisco, CA 94111-4696
Tel: 415-772-4430
Fax: 415-391-9929
www.ncccsf.org

community realize economies of scale while preserving multiple strategies to address problems.

- By fostering community examination of needed systems changes, the infrastructure makes apparent the tools needed for successful collaboration, including the need for technology to support collaborative work and system-based outcomes measurement.

- By tracking the community's return on investment in social services, the infrastructure provides information that allows budgeting and implementation to focus on prevention rather than remediation.

- By holding all members of the community to high aspirations for achievement, the infrastructure provides an ongoing stimulus for community improvement. It makes possible the citizen engagement that moves social challenges from problems to be addressed by nonprofits and government to solutions to be enabled by the full community.

Funding a Supportive Infrastructure

How can funders help to ensure that a community has access to some form of supportive infrastructure? The answer involves much more than funding. Because this infrastructure occupies that uncharted territory between organization boundaries, and must always act and be perceived as an impartial intermediary for collaboration, both the structure and the role of funding are hard to define. Where will the support specialists come from and where will they be housed? Will this be their full-time responsibility? Will they have their own organization or be interwoven with the community systems they serve? How will the work of support *people* be enabled by the support *resources* of information technology and community data?

And how will funds be made available to pay for this? To be effective in their role, support specialists cannot afford to let funding shape their priorities in the community. Funding cannot, for example, lead them into program delivery, or they will simply be seen as one more service provider. Funds also cannot come with so many strings attached that they prevent support specialists from responding flexibly to the needs of collaboratives and the unexpected twists and turns of community work. And funding should not come from only one source, because that would allow a single funder too much influence over decisions that must be the whole community's to make.

Ideally, a supportive infrastructure should be funded by a collaborative of local private and public funding sources, as well as national funding when possible. Rather than the community having to piece together a patchwork of funding opportunities (and all the separate accounting and reporting that goes with them), a funder collaborative can pool resources on behalf of the community into a single grant. We suggest that such funding could be used to

- Support the salaries of support specialists in various collaboratives
- Support the design and operations of a new community support organization
- Support the process of evolving a community support organization from an existing organization

Fund support specialists in various collaboratives

The most obvious way to fund support for community problem solving is to ensure that each collaborative has the money to pay one or more individuals to provide the kinds of support services we have described. Many collaborative groups already target some of their funding to this, whether to pay the partial salary of an employee of one of the group's members (so that part of his or her job duties can be to serve the group) or to hire a dedicated assistant. This is a reasonable starting point for funders who want to do something to meet the support needs of community problem solving.

Our experience shows, however, that this approach has drawbacks:

- The support staff may not be perceived as neutral players, because they are also committed to the work of one participating organization in the collaborative.
- They may not be specialists in many aspects of meaningful support, such as facilitation, conflict resolution, and bridge building.

- They often do not have the time necessary to continually engage more members of the community or to follow up on research needs between meetings.

- They cannot turn to a community infrastructure to bridge their own collaborative with other community work.

- They may not have the leadership clout to hold the group to its highest aspirations.

- They may find themselves keeping support tasks to a minimum of secretarial duties that can be delegated to an administrative assistant.

By itself, funding support specialists for individual collaborations does not, in our opinion, constitute a supportive infrastructure. The potential to transform community work into effective solutions to complex problems is limited.

Fund a community support organization

All our study in the last several years on how communities could be helped to succeed with systems change, and how funders could have greater impact on complex problems, has always come back to the need for support. But the more we learned about the importance of impartial support and ever-widening circles of community engagement, the more we were challenged to envision how this support could be structured within that uncharted territory between sectors of society. So we looked to communities for examples that seemed to meet all the requirements revealed by our research. We found a few dedicated local organizations that house and provide resources for support staff. They represent a true infrastructure of support that crosses boundaries, builds bridges, and serves multiple community efforts.

A community support organization (CSO) is an impartial, skilled, local intermediary dedicated to fostering the success of local collaborations and systemic reforms in order to improve the way the community solves problems.

We coined the term *community support organization* to describe this kind of infrastructure.[31] We defined a community support organization (CSO) as an impartial, skilled, local intermediary dedicated to fostering the success of local collaborations and systemic reforms in order to improve the way the

66

community solves problems. Sidebars in this chapter profile examples of what we mean by a community support organization. Because the concept is new, however, few communities can currently turn to a community support organization (or similar structure) to support their collaborative efforts.

While the community support organization need not be a newly created organization in the community, it must be housed in an accessible, impartial, and well-respected local entity. In addition, to fully leverage the benefits of this infrastructure, it should not be designed with a specific community collaboration in mind; instead, it should be designed to serve multiple systemic efforts. The staff of the community support organization would provide all the supportive services discussed in this chapter, while building bridges across collaborative groups and with policy makers and other community-wide decision makers.

Ideally, the services of a community support organization are applied to various collaborative efforts as needed. Just as a movie's behind-the-scenes technical and design support increases with the complexity of the film, so the services of the community support organization ebb and flow with the complexity of the community collaborations. Some may require a full complement of services, from convening to research to logistical assistance to managing funds, while others may simply need regular administrative support. The community support organization may support existing collaborative groups or help start new collaborations around emerging concerns.

Because the community support organization serves the entire community, we recommend that decisions about how it will be used should be overseen by some kind of community governance body, whether the board of an existing organization that is evolving into a community support organization, or a newly created community forum that represents the desires of the community at large (See Appendix, Community Governance Strategies). Whatever kind of governing body is used, it must ensure that the community support organization remains a servant to the community, even as it may behave as a leader for the process of collaboration. community support organization staff would convene regular meetings of this community forum to report on the work of the community support organization and ask for guidance. The community forum would be responsible for prioritizing services and ensuring that the community support organization has adequate resources to accomplish its tasks. Ideally, the community forum would include representatives from the various collaborative governance bodies that guide improvement of each community system. Figure 3 shows how one community support organization might relate to the various collaborations it supports.

Figure 3. The Community Support Organization in Its Local Context

Community Forum
Represents the desires of the community at large. Participants are from all sectors and include key decision makers. The forum always has an empty chair for new participants.

Funders Standing Committee

Sustainability Community Planning Committee

Continuum of Care Community

Community Support Organization

Youth at Risk Planning Team

Independence Board

Arts and Culture Coalition

Future Systems Work

Community Health Board

Workforce Investment Board

Future Collaborations

The community support organization acts as a servant to the community even as it sometimes leads the process of collaboration. This example shows a community support organization providing services to a number of collaborations and systems within the community.

Support the design and operations of a new community support organization.
Funders and other community leaders may want to create a new organization to supply supportive services. Designing a new community support
organization has the advantage of a blank slate—it carries no history, con-
ventions, or negative baggage that could affect its impartiality or ability to
make support services its priority. On the other hand, a new community
support organization may face greater barriers to community buy-in than
an existing organization with an established budget and leadership.

The following steps will need to be taken in order to design a new organization:

- Convene a conversation with broad community engagement
- Involve leaders of existing multisector collaborations
- Find meeting space that is considered neutral territory
- Facilitate the meetings to both encourage involvement and challenge
  participants to aspire
- Bring together multiple local funders to commit their support
- Create a community governing body to oversee the community support
  organization
- Communicate regularly and clearly to the larger community about the
  plans for a community support organization
- Complete all paperwork to establish a new organizational entity
- Hire staff for the community support organization who are well-
  respected, multiskilled, and perceived as impartial
- Locate and equip work space for the community support organization
  staff
- Train community support organization staff to be servant-leaders for
  collaborative groups

The persons who take on these tasks can be from any sector of the community, but the ideal would be a partnership of business, government,
nonprofit, and neighborhood representatives. Leadership from a local or

national funder (or funder collaborative) can be particularly valuable at this stage, since the design of a community support organization requires collaboration even before services are up and running. By providing seed funding and convening relevant players, funders can enable the community to overcome the initial barriers to putting a community support organization in place.

Support the process of evolving a community support organization from an existing organization. The development of community support organization services in a community often will not occur in the simple fashion just described. While some communities may design a community support organization from scratch (for an example in Kansas City, see the sidebar in Chapter Two on page 40), others may evolve community support organizations from existing organizations, such as planning councils, community foundations, or nonprofit management support organizations.[32] The advantages of this evolutionary process are the ability to respond more quickly to the demand for services, to use equipment and space that have already been invested in the community, to slowly develop services as needs arise, and to avoid the critical attention that a new organization often gets.

On the other hand, an existing organization has a history that may affect its impartial stance in the community, and its board and staff may not as easily take to their new roles as people specifically recruited for supportive services. In many ways, the risks of turning an organization into a community support organization are similar to the problems that an organization faces when trying to become the lead agency in a collaboration. Funders can assist the process of evolving an existing organization into a community support organization by sponsoring orientations and training for board members and staff, enabling additional staff to be hired as necessary, supporting a communications plan, and encouraging broad community engagement.

Whether the community gets a new community support organization or develops one out of an existing organization, adequate funding to support the work of serving multiple community collaboratives will be needed.

Funds for a community support organization are difficult to secure in a traditional funding environment that requires choosing between direct-service grants and capacity-building efforts. Funders must value community capacity building, successful collaboration, and systems change in their funding plans, as long as this work focuses on solutions. And community collaboratives must be creative in thinking about how to use new grant opportunities to enhance their ability to work together to solve problems.

Strategic Benefits of the Community Support Organization

At first blush, it may appear that the community support organization is simply an additional cost for the community. However, if funders are willing to invest in the community support organization and the tools necessary for reforming systems of services, the community support organization can provide returns on this investment in the form of greater efficiency and cost reductions. Many of the suggestions earlier in this book about funding management information systems, systemwide outcomes measurement, and research data for better decision making are made possible through the infrastructure of the community support organization. For example, the community support organization can coordinate the process of selecting, customizing, implementing, and maintaining a management information system across multiple agencies that will bring new insights about client use, redundancies and gaps in service, funding allocations, and system design.

When such tools are implemented, the community can see where the system can be improved, where funding can be leveraged more strategically, and where services can be streamlined. Unlike calls for mergers and acquisitions to reduce duplication, the tools for systemic improvement—made possible by advances in technology and enabled by the community support organization—allow the community to start with its goals and know what to change to reach these goals without eliminating strategies. Thus, funders

Impact takes its most positive form when problems are not only solved but also prevented. By funding systems and community work—and supporting this work through an infrastructure like a community support organization— foundations have the best chance of seeing their work lead to prevention.

can stop throwing money at problems, and communities can bring greater wisdom to using their funding.

At the start of this book, we talked about the funder's desire to have a positive impact. Impact takes its most positive form when problems are not only solved but also prevented. By funding systems and community work—and supporting this work through an infrastructure like a community support organization—foundations have the best chance of seeing their work lead to prevention, because savings from better-designed community systems can be reinvested in preventive services.[33] But without an intermediary at the systems level to negotiate more flexible use of funds, to ensure documentation of improved outcomes and cost savings, and to facilitate community discussions of how to prevent problems, the challenges of redirecting funds and focusing on preventive services are unlikely to be overcome. Funding community support organizations over the long term is an investment not only in the community's capacity to solve problems but also in the community's ability to avert problems altogether.

Strategic Disadvantages of the Community Support Organization

We believe the community support organization is a powerful tool for funders to leverage resources to solve problems and have a positive impact in communities. While the examples we have studied have not pointed to many disadvantages of this approach, community support organizations have also not been around long enough for a full understanding of the pros and cons. For one thing, asking a community to invest in a community support organization assumes that the community is already trying out various efforts to work at a systems level and can see the benefits of a coordinating infrastructure. If the community is, however, still struggling to get to this point, the community support organization could easily appear inappropriate. Other possible risks may include

- Drawing funds away from immediate care services that communities must still provide while searching for systemic solutions

- Exacerbating the sense of competition for limited resources, if local nonprofits are not already working at a systems level together

- Creating an unhealthy dependence on the community support organization at times when organizations should be investing in solving their own conflicts

- Requiring the community support organization to get involved in programmatic services in order to keep its funding

- Investing key networking knowledge in a few people—concentrating important relationships in a few individuals whose loss would decimate the fabric of multiple collaborations and informal arrangements

- Appearing as a threat to local government if the community support organization role is not clearly defined

Funders As Community Support Organizations

Another way in which funders can enable the community to access CSO-type services is by providing these services themselves. A local community foundation, United Way office, or private foundation can target staff and resources to serving multiple local collaboratives. Or a national funder might explore this role, either in the community where it is located, or with multiple communities that it funds, as long as a permanent local presence is available to meet the daily needs of community work.

Just as when funding another organization to be a community support organization, any funder that wants to assume this role will have to ensure the community's buy-in and acceptance of those providing services. There are several advantages to having a funder serve as a community support organization:

- By providing community support organization services, the funder demonstrates its commitment to the value of collaboration, to the community's aspirations, and to the long-term investments needed to reach them.

- Local funders bring broad knowledge of the local nonprofit sector and ongoing programs that could be folded into collaborative efforts.

- Funders usually have the clout to bring leaders to the table.

- Working directly with collaboratives allows the funder to develop in-depth knowledge of the system and its challenges, and increases the incentives for the funder to help the community access resources.

- Funders see firsthand the value of funding capacity building and the tools for systemic work.

- Acting as a community support organization strengthens the local funder's position as a community leader and community servant.

- Funders often have the influence to speak and advocate for community needs and ideas with levels of government outside of the community.

Of course, these advantages are available to foundations whether or not they directly provide CSO-type services. While community support organization work can be enhanced by these funder strengths, taking on the role of community support organization also presents risks to the funder:

- All participants in community collaboratives must perceive the community support organization as an impartial intermediary whose only agenda is to get the community from where it is now to its highest aspirations. If a funder serves as a community support organization, it must exude and continually demonstrate this impartial role. This can be difficult in an environment where funders come into a meeting and say, "Good morning," and everyone responds with "Good point."[34]

- If a funder appears to have a leadership role in collaborations, other funders may think that their involvement and resources are unnecessary or unwelcome.

- The funder's board and executive leadership may not value the long-term investment and staff time spent on providing intensive, hands-on services to the community. This is a much different role from donor cultivation, funds management, grantmaking, or setting priorities for resource allocation.

- If the funder evolves into a community support organization role to serve the needs of a specific collaboration, it may begin to see this work as a pet project and not recognize the support needs of other community collaboratives.

- A national funder trying to serve as a local community support organization may not have enough local knowledge or local presence to ensure adequate services to the ongoing, unexpected, and sometimes very particular challenges of community-level work.

A Funder as a Community Support Organization: Hands-On Support from a Community Foundation

Since 1994, San Mateo County, California, has had the benefit of a community collaboration called the Peninsula Partnership for Children, Youth, and Families.[35] This partnership has linked public and private resources and leadership to improve kindergarten readiness and reading proficiency among third graders as key goals for enhancing the lives of children and youth and preventing future problems. Using a simultaneous bottom-up and top-down approach, a governing body called the Partnership Council (which consists of leaders from city and county government, schools, nonprofits, and foundations) helps nine local collaboratives as they build networks and strengthen strategies (such as home visiting

for new parents and preschool book-lending programs) to reach the core goals.

Early in the development of the Peninsula Partnership, participants recognized the need for "full-time glue" to support community work, says Sterling Speirn, president of the Peninsula Community Foundation, which helped initiate the Partnership Council. "We know collaboration doesn't take place on the backs of everybody's full-time job." The Partnership Council responded by hiring a full-time director who became a staff person of the Peninsula Community Foundation, but who was directly accountable to the Partnership Council with daily responsibility to serve and facilitate its work.

Over time, three additional staff have been added, and Speirn commits about 15 percent of his time directly to Partnership Council work. In this way, he says, the foundation emulates "the idea of a community support organization" with the staff going to meetings all over the county and "just being out there to make it all happen."

The director of the Peninsula Partnership, Jennifer Sedbrook, and her staff are responsible for a variety of supportive activities, including orienting new Partnership Council members to its history and purpose, recruiting and training community residents to get involved in the local collaboratives, preparing agendas and reports for collaborative meetings, exploring new early childhood initiatives that might help meet its goals, convening and facilitating task forces to pursue new initiatives, helping local community collaboratives access funds for various programs, and negotiating the connection between the Peninsula Community Foundation and the Partnership Council.

Sedbrook continually reminds herself that "It's communication, stupid!" as she regularly distributes meeting minutes and calls individual participants to make sure they feel connected to any new idea that the Partnership Council is considering. She emphasizes that the neutral position of the Partnership Council (compared to any one participating organization) "elevates the status" of any new opportunity, "taking it out of the political realm" and allowing the community to get things done.

It has required unusual "foundation stamina," says Speirn, for the Peninsula Community Foundation to commit itself to such a comprehensive, long-term community effort, but the results have been worth it. For example, the county health department reorganized itself to focus more on prenatal-to-age-three services, a book-bag program now sends books home each day to over 15,000 preschoolers, and significant changes have been made in the culture and habits of local problem solving, allowing some communities to leverage millions of new dollars on behalf of children and families. "We're not here for ourselves," says Speirn about the Peninsula Community Foundation. "We say our job is to realize the philanthropic dreams of our community, whether those dreams are held by a donor, or a nonprofit leader, or a school teacher, or a principal."

Supporting the Peninsula Partnership, he adds, continues to bring "rich information and relationships" to the foundation, allowing its board and staff to truly know the communities it serves and bring innovative opportunities to its donors and grantmaking decisions.

For more information, contact:
The Peninsula Partnership for Children, Youth, and Families
The Peninsula Community Foundation
1700 South El Camino Real, Suite 300
San Mateo, CA 94402-3049
Tel: 650-358-8922
Fax: 650-358-0141
www.pcf.org

Community Support Organization Dos and Don'ts

The value of a community support organization lies in its ability to lead and serve simultaneously, to be neutral while at the same time challenging everyone to high aspirations, to work in uncharted territory between boundaries while remaining relevant to all sectors. Our research and experiences have demonstrated that these dual responsibilities can be tricky to balance, leading to procedural or policy recommendations that, at first glance, might seem counterintuitive. Some suggestions for the staff and governing body of a community support organization include the following:

1. DO focus everyone's attention on the highest aspirations for the community. The galvanizing force of a problem-solving vision not only will secure your most passionate early participants but also will serve to engage, over time, broader sections of the community.

2. DON'T let discussions revolve around least-common-denominator agreements. Your community deserves better than uninspired efforts at consensus. If it's easy, it's probably not sufficient.

3. DO post on the meeting room wall the goal and the process to achieve that goal. Continuous reminders of both the goal and process keep discussions on task and serve as a quick orientation for guests or new members.

4. DO ensure that each collaborative group develops and adheres to guiding principles (or "nonnegotiables") and group norms.

5. DON'T be a passive facilitator of collaborative meetings. Being neutral is not the same as being passive. The community support organization has a point of view, which is squarely focused on achieving the community's goals and solving the problems. Its facilitation may well be neutral as to methods and means, but not to expectations. Challenge participants to rise to the occasion.

6. DO evaluate every collaborative meeting and share results with participants. No meeting is worth having if you are not evaluating whether its objectives were met. This evaluation need not be lengthy or time-con-

suming. It can be as simple as a three-question survey that asks both ongoing, "pulse-taking" questions to build trust and maintain momentum (How would you assess your participation in tonight's meeting?) and questions that underscore goals or requirements (How would you rate today's meeting for increasing our understanding of this issue?). An evaluation also provides a confidential forum for participants to express concerns that can arise at each meeting.

7. DO provide safe harbors for stakeholders to explore their positions before going public. In an open community forum, it is natural for a group of providers or funders or other stakeholders to feel the need to defend their past actions. This defense focuses on points of contention rather than points of agreement. The larger progress toward a shared aspiration can get stuck or derailed if the stakeholders aren't given a chance to deal with disagreements outside the spotlight of a community forum.

8. DON'T let the group be held hostage to "those who should be here." Collaboratives usually get stuck early in the process because the desire to get everyone around the table supersedes discussion of goals. While community engagement should be ongoing, those who are already participating should not wait to begin their work toward shared aspirations.

9. DO develop an expectation for broader and broader community participation.

10. DO keep an "open chair" at all meetings. By this we mean being open to new members and committing the collaborative and community support organization staff to orient and support whoever sits in the chair.

11. DON'T let the need to build trust keep groups from taking action. A classic passive-aggressive posture to keeping the status quo is to embrace change but delay action by a need to build trust. No better foundation for ongoing trust could be laid than by taking successful action, together.

12. DO expect the collaborative to test all proposed actions against the goal or aspiration. There is no easier way for a group to get hijacked to irrelevance than to act on meaningless or marginal items. The time, tal-

ent, and passion of the members of a collaborative are rare and fleeting resources. Invest them wisely.

13. DON'T let a perceived lack of resources curtail the group's aspirations. How the work is organized must take precedence over funding matters because, until you see the path to where you are going, much money can be wasted in wrong turns. Conversely, once the path is clear, many new sources of support can present themselves.

14. DO provide well-organized research and data (for example, practices from other communities) to inform decision making. The community support organization must provide information—normative and strategic—to enable intelligent decisions. But it must also be mindful not to inundate or confuse.

15. DON'T be led into capacity building for individual organizations. Be clear that the community support organization's focus is on systems change for community solutions. Technical assistance for individual organizations is necessary for strengthening a community, but providing such services is work for others. The work of the community support organization is across organizations and sectors.

16. DON'T confuse respect with low expectations. For a collaborative to achieve its goals, each participating organization will be expected to change the way it does its work and interacts with other organizations. A balance must be struck between preserving individual strategies while holding everyone to standards that will ensure the community's desired outcomes are accomplished.

17. DO expect the collaborative to set deadlines and keep to them. Engagement, momentum, and achievement are all more likely if there is a creative pressure to keep moving.

18. DON'T underestimate the value of technology. Failed efforts at collaboration are often blamed on lack of information, communication, and follow-through. New technologies can alleviate these potential pitfalls as never before.

19. DON'T underestimate the need for widespread participation in all stages of implementing new technology. Potential users at all levels of the system must be included in planning, design, and deployment.

20. DO prepare community support organization staff and governance bodies for balancing the servant-leader and facilitator-challenger roles. All the other dos and don'ts depend on skilled support, leadership, and service.

A Community Support Organization in Action:
High Aspirations Lead to Greater Resources

While exploring the work of CSO-type organizations in other communities, the Collaboratory for Community Support sought to experience firsthand the value of community support services in one local community. Combining its own resources with funds from the City Council of Toledo, Ohio, the Collaboratory began facilitating and coaching a community-wide effort to address homelessness through a comprehensive, coordinated approach. It served as an impartial convener, researcher, meeting facilitator, and connector for the people involved in the homelessness project. (While the Collaboratory was demonstrating CSO-type services, its offices were not located in Toledo, so its story does not fully illustrate how the community support organization can be a total community resource.)

The Collaboratory began its efforts in the fall of 1999 by bringing together a broadly representative community body that learned about homelessness in the community. In addition to reading research reports, the community body developed its knowledge by listening to presentations by representatives of other local groups—of service providers, clients, and funders—whom the Collaboratory had also convened separately to assist in preparing their presentations. The larger community body then developed a shared goal and recommendations for addressing homelessness in Toledo that represent the community's highest aspirations. With the Collaboratory's assistance, this community group has since moved forward on a variety of tasks, including creating a permanent governing body for the homeless

An Emerging Need

In Chapter Two, we briefly mentioned a decision by the Northwest Area Foundation to restructure its giving practices from short-term funding for selected communities to long-term grants for systemic problem solving. Since that change began in early 2000, the foundation has noticed an emerging trend in the community processes that are now under way. While not using the term community support organization, the communities—from rural Miner County, South Dakota, to urban Minneapolis—are

services system and exploring options for the purchase of a multiorganization management information system. In addition, the circle of participants from throughout the community has continued to widen (to over 150 people), allowing a greater understanding of the problem and a greater representation of those who can influence policy, resources, and services to get results.

The value of this participation was evident when the new governing body was reviewing Toledo's 2000 "Continuum of Care" application to HUD for funding for homelessness services. With the diligent review of community members and attention to their highest aspirations for the community, the governing body was able to develop enhanced strategies and increase the grant request by 25 percent over the prior year. HUD granted the funds, thus providing Toledo with greater resources to apply to a more coordinated approach. The

behind-the-scenes facilitation by the CSO-like Collaboratory resulted in funding for Toledo's highest aspirations for resolving the issues of homelessness.

For more information, contact:
The Collaboratory for Community Support
2410 Newport Road
Ann Arbor, MI 48103
Tel: 734-623-4952
Fax: 734-741-9223
e-mail: JCRubicon@aol.com
www.comnet.org/collaboratorycs/

calling out for some kind of supportive infrastructure, some well-defined and specifically dedicated coordinating entity to do the hands-on work of managing community-wide efforts. As they undertake the visioning, action steps, and evaluation plans for change, an undeniable groundswell of need for CSO-type services is being independently identified by various communities.

The Northwest Area Foundation is beginning to create community support organizations to fill this need. While such behind-the-scenes support is not the only requirement for successful community problem solving, we believe it is an essential tool. In the next chapter, we discuss strategies that foundations can employ to begin the process of "being the change they wish to see," supporting communities in solving problems.

A Process to Lay the Groundwork for Change

IN CHAPTER ONE, WE SUGGESTED THAT THE TIME AND CIRCUMstances are ideal for foundations to fund successful community problem solving. In Chapter Two, we outlined strategies for funding solutions. And in Chapter Three, we discussed methods for sustaining community problem-solving efforts. We emphasized developing infrastructures like community support organizations—local resources that provide the "glue and connective tissue" for problem-solving work in communities across North America.

In this chapter, we share process lessons for getting from here to there—lessons we learned while working with foundations. We discuss the internal and external changes that foundations consider as they evaluate where they want to be on a continuum from individual program support to fostering successful community problem solving. As we said at the outset of this book, funders want what communities want—a positive impact on the problem, a solution. But what a positive impact means and how it plays out in the funder's daily decisions can be conflicting and often confusing. From the point of view of the various stakeholders—program officers, grantees, foundation board members, community leaders, and so forth—the situation is similar to that of the proverbial three blindfolded men around the elephant: It appears to be a dramatically different beast depending on where you are standing.

For this reason, we have developed the model shown in Figure 4. At the heart of the model is a three-step process that seeks to align perspectives of the various stakeholders and thereby leverage resources for greater positive impact. The three steps in that process are

1. Know the present
2. Encourage aspiration
3. Identify infrastructure requirements

Figure 4. A Process for Laying the Groundwork for Change

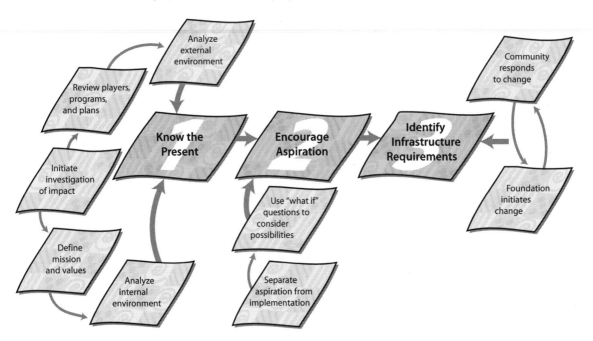

Know the Present

Foundations that want to change the way they support community problem solving begin by examining their present ways of thinking and acting. Though the foundation's strategic plan, mission, and values statements are good jumping-off points for this reflection, the intent here is to develop new insights around the desire for impact—both personally and organizationally. Psychologists refer to the gap between what one wants to do and what one is doing as *dissonance*. The first step in laying the groundwork for change—know the present—identifies the degree of personal and organizational dissonance that accompanies the foundation's present means of operation. The greater this dissonance, the greater the motivation for change.

Knowing the present requires two simultaneous considerations: internal and external. *Internal considerations* are often thought of as strengths and weaknesses. However, in this examination the foundation should drill deeply into the strengths and weaknesses in its underlying functions and skills rather than the static structures and policies typically examined in a strategic plan. The foundation needs to understand its capacity to achieve a given function, not simply how it has been organized to perform that function. For example, the foundation may discover that the process for disbursing grant dollars meets auditing requirements but impedes the timely provision of resources to the community. Understanding and celebrating core competencies can ignite an enthusiasm for change, whereas spotlighting structure can maintain inertia against change.

External considerations involve the community that the foundation is trying to assist. This environmental scan could include a trend analysis: How fragmented are the services? What kinds of collaboration are being tried? However, the foundation must be clear about the contours of the community its work encompasses. Be it a geographic, ideological, or other community, its identity, parameters, and boundaries must be defined and understood. A full external analysis should also account for all the players, programs, and plans already in place.

Foundations can use many different methods—breakout sessions, focus groups, community surveys, and so forth—to develop insight about the present internal and external environments in which change must occur. But the relevant questions regarding impact are fairly straightforward:

Internally:

1. What are the ...
   a. Values
   b. Goals
   c. Measurements
   d. Barriers
   e. Benefits

   ...of the present method our foundation uses to set grantmaking guidelines?

2. What are our organizational "givens"—written or ingrained? Do these cultural norms or policies continue to reflect who we are or should be?

3. What are our core competencies—the two to five things we do best?

4. Do we view our role as building the capacity of individuals within the community to do the work of supporting collaboration? If so, how will we see that the work can continue when we are no longer involved?

5. Have we changed our definition of success? Why or why not? How?

6. How do we manifest leadership—do we have a servant, hierarchical, or catalytic style?

7. Where would we place ourselves on the continuum from individual program support to fostering successful community problem solving?

8. What is the foundation's definition of community?

9. How can we respect the traditions and methods that have served the foundation well in the past while moving to new traditions and methods?

10. How would we assess our board's ability to accept change?

11. If change were desired, who would need to be involved in the decision?

Externally:

12. What have our efforts achieved in the community? Are we satisfied?

13. How have our past successes changed the nature of the problem we are still addressing?

14. What difficulties do our grantees face in translating our expectations into real outcomes?

15. What is the "cost" of our requirements to grantees, to their clients, or to both?

16. What is our relationship with our current grantees? How different are the answers to this question depending on whom we ask?

17. How do we currently use our relationships and networks to achieve our goals? What changes are needed to address community problems?

18. Who are the key players—individual and organizational—and what are the programs and plans at work in our targeted community? What is our desired relationship to each?

19. What are the opportunities for and threats to leveraging impact on community systems and solutions?

20. How can whatever we do be sustained?

21. Have we discussed with other funders (public or private) the opportunities for leverage or collaboration? With which funders have we created partnerships?

22. With which additional funders (public or private) or institutional stakeholders should we discuss these opportunities if our goal is to achieve sustainable solutions?

This series of questions is not prescriptive and not meant to lead you to a preordained conclusion. The questions are fashioned to help you and your foundation create a picture of the present as it involves your foundation, your community, and your role and relationships in the community. Knowing this present, warts and all, is vital in preparing to create what's possible—in being able to act on your aspirations.

Encourage Aspiration

Vision without action is a daydream;
action without vision is a nightmare.
—Japanese Proverb

Once the foundation has developed a good sense of itself and its community by knowing the present, it can turn to the next step in the process: encouraging aspiration. As we have emphasized in this book, one of the core strategies for funding solutions is challenging the community to aspire. If the foundation is to guide and insist on this in the community, it is only reasonable that the foundation itself model this capability. The authors of *The Dance of Change* find that the ability to aspire is present in all organizations that generate and sustain profound change. They define aspiration as "the capability to orient, individually and collectively, toward creating what people truly desire, rather than just reacting to circumstances."[36]

While it may be presumptuous to generalize from our experience, we have observed that the reaction to an offer to aspire is uniform and consistent. Whether we are working with a foundation team, a diverse group of service providers, a class of graduate students, or a gathering of community residents, when we encourage participants to aspire, they always respond with the following: "There is clearly a better way." And then, "But there is [this and that external reason or reasons] why we can't get there." We have facilitated enough organizational and group efforts to achieve collective aspirations that we can report that the former insight is almost always true, while the latter seldom is.

Because of inertia, most organizations and communities rarely confront the falsity of the reasons they give for why something can't be accomplished. "We are just so darn busy coping … and that's the way it's always been." Thus, absent crisis, organizations, including foundations, typically need to give themselves permission—make a formal intention—to develop aspirations for themselves and their communities. To aspire, foundations must think in a different way, ask the unasked, discuss the undiscussable. To encourage aspiration, foundations can use a broad range of methods—brainstorming exercises, community circles, breakout sessions, focus groups, surveys, and so forth—to lay the groundwork for change. A series of "what if" questions can be used during these sessions:

1. What if we funded communities rather than programs?

2. What if we funded systems rather than organizations?

3. What if community systems could each be managed like an enterprise? What infrastructure would they require to be successful?

4. What if we could do anything to achieve positive impact? Would we do something differently than what we are doing now?

5. What if our grantees were given a choice about how they worked with us? Would they structure their grants (expectations, measurements, evaluations, reporting, and so forth) the way we presently do?

6. What if we were confronting our foundation's major causes for the first time? Would we organize our response the same way as we presently address the issues?

The word *aspiration* is derived from the Latin for breathing—a basic act of life. Yet, people often have great difficulty articulating their aspirations, let alone acting on them. These six questions help you and your foundation gauge the gap between articulation and action. In a manner nearly as reflexive as breathing, people often preempt this visualization because all they see are the reasons things "can't be done." By separating the act of aspiring from that of implementing, you can create a powerful picture of what is possible and necessary to achieve solutions in your community. This fully conceived aspiration then has the power to shift your perceptions of barriers into actionable changes in infrastructure that will make implementation possible.

Identify Infrastructure Requirements

The final process step in beginning to move along the continuum from individual program support to fostering successful community problem solving has to do with the competencies, information, resources, practices, standards, procedures, and structures needed to channel activity in new directions. These constitute the infrastructure required to reach the aspirations identified in the previous step. The internal and external tasks undertaken to meet these infrastructure requirements indicate how far and at what speed the foundation moves across the continuum.

Infrastructure is the means through which an organization makes available resources (including human resources) to support people in their work. It might include new systems for measuring outcomes, new governance structures, new forums for convening collaborative groups, new management information systems, new research methods, and new communication devices for community engagement. In our experience, the single-most-likely cause for failure of a new initiative is the failure to develop an accompanying infrastructure.

In this book, we have discussed infrastructure from two vantage points: (1) within the foundation (Chapter Two's section Be the Change You Wish to See); and (2) within the community (Chapter Three's discussion of the support services that sustain community problem solving).

As your foundation reviews these opportunities for new internal and external infrastructures, keep in mind that in actual practice, where successful, these changes are typically not made independently or sequentially—first the foundation, then the community, or vice versa. Instead, moving through the continuum is typically an interactive process. The foundation initiates a change, to which the community responds, to which the foundation adapts, and so on.

The foundation and the community will need to consider infrastructure issues such as the following in order to achieve community solutions:

1. *Funding approaches:* How are funds for community solutions to be held, leveraged, and distributed? What funding approaches beside individual program grants are possible:

   - Donor-advised funds?

   - A sponsoring organization?

   - A partnership with a local funder?

   - Comingling public and private funds?

   Is a competitive grantmaking process still appropriate? Are grant proposals still necessary? Could foundation staff and community members write the grant-spending plan together?

2. *Governance:* What kind of community governance will meet the expectations of funders and community members:

   - A community advisory forum?

   - The board of a new 501(c)(3)?

   - The board of an existing community institution?

   How will this governance reflect the community's full diversity, be perceived as neutral, and continue to engage broader circles of constituents?

3. *Role:* How will the foundation interact with the community? What new roles will be expected of foundation staff, executives, and board members:

   - A community coach?

   - An information provider?

   - An information manager?

   - The staff of a community support organization?

   - An equal partner with other community representatives?

4. *Neutrality:* How will neutrality be manifest in the community's work:

   - Finding a consistent and neutral meeting place?

   - Reflecting all sectors—nonprofit, government, and business?

- Developing rules for decision making to avoid conflicts of interest?
- Keeping the community's highest aspirations in the forefront of all actions?

5. *Sustainability:* What mechanisms will ensure sustainability of the effort:

- Involvement of all key institutions?
- Ongoing measurement of the larger community's perceptions, reactions, and aspirations (through surveys, focus groups, and so forth)?
- Instituting a supporting infrastructure to accomplish behind-the-scenes tasks?

6. *Effectiveness*: What mechanisms will ensure ongoing learning, evaluation, and training:

- Regularly obtaining research results on best practices?
- Assessing community success indicators and outcomes?
- Networking with other communities?
- Archiving lessons learned, "community memory," and "foundation memory"?

We have emphasized the value of a community support organization as one kind of infrastructure that could answer some of these questions and foster comprehensive solutions. Creating such a multifaceted resource requires changes both internally at foundations and externally throughout the community. Whatever approaches to new infrastructure are taken, foundations can take a lead role in moving everyone along the continuum toward solutions. The work involved in laying the groundwork for change—knowing the present, aspiring, and putting in place the necessary infrastructure—is certainly challenging for foundations. It will require the savvy and subtlety of servant leadership at its best. But foundations that embrace the challenge also embrace the opportunity for positive change for themselves and those they serve.

Conclusion:
Our Aspiration for You

We shall not cease from exploration
And the end of all our exploring
Will be to arrive where we started
And know the place for the first time.
  —*T.S. Eliot,* Four Quartets *(1943)*

WE ARE FORTUNATE IN THE UNITED STATES TO HAVE A strong tradition of philanthropy and a large and varied foundation community eager to give and to serve. Many social successes and opportunities can be directly tied to the work that foundations have been doing for decades. But everyone wants to do better with what they have, make their resources go farther, see more of a positive impact, and know that their commitment, day in and day out, is making a difference. As the authors of this book and, like you, change agents in our communities, we hope we have provided you with some fresh ideas, practical suggestions, and immediate steps that you can take to encourage, enable, and be a part of community problem solving. And we hope that, if you have taken the exploratory trek of reading this book and now find yourself here at the end, you are actually finding yourself at the beginning of a new journey in your work that will be satisfying, uplifting, and successful.

Appendix: Community Governance Strategies

The Appendix offers several options for structuring a community governance entity to oversee the work of improving a community. While not an exhaustive list, it outlines a range of choices available to a community, and the pros and cons of each choice. As communities consider their governance options, they may also think about evolving the governance structure from one form to another over its life cycle.

Government Committee

A body of local leaders convened by local government and charged with raising awareness but with no formal mandate, policy authority, or direct access to resources.

Pros:
- Easy and inexpensive to establish
- Can bring community focus to the seriousness of a problem and the need for solutions
- Able to affect policy through direct channels

Cons:
- Dependent on government bureaucracy
- Little authority to change practices within system

Volunteer Committee

A group of community leaders, self-selected or invited but not directly affiliated with any organization or sector, that recommends and oversees systems changes and accountability to community goals.

Pros:
- Creates broad community engagement
- Federal mandates are looking for more of this kind of governance
- Committee can also inform and oversee systems change for other social problems

Cons:
- Committee is not part of members' jobs; this can affect commitment and attendance and limits expertise on issues
- Authority is limited unless specifically outlined and agreed upon by others in the system
- No direct access to resources

501(c)(3)

An independent nonprofit organization, with its own board of directors, charged with overseeing systems change, coordinating services, collecting data, or raising and regranting funds.

Pros:
- Gives immediate, concrete focus to community goal and actions
- Creates a legal entity to receive funds, hire staff, maintain governing board, and be accountable

Cons:
- Costly to operate
- Can become too internally focused, forgetting community goals in favor of survival and control
- Has to be either a membership or directorship organization

Government Office

A department within city or county government charged with overseeing systems change, coordinating services, collecting data, or raising and regranting funds.

Pros:
- Gives immediate, concrete focus to community goals and actions
- Creates a government entity capable of raising tax-based funds
- Creates direct relationship between federal fiduciary and governing board
- Carries authority for planning and implementation

Cons:
- Effectiveness depends on public opinion and community engagement
- Existence depends on favor of political "in-group"
- Unwieldy bureaucratic processes may get in the way
- Limits funding opportunities from certain source

Cross-Organization Collaboration

An ongoing collaborative alliance among leaders of organizations within the system. May be a (1) collaboration of providers, (2) collaboration of funders, or (3) collaboration of institution leaders.

Pros:

- Brings together experts on the problem to plan solutions
- Allows for ever-increasing membership of organizations that can impact the problem

Cons:

- Each group by itself does not have full authority to change the system

(1) Collaboration of Providers

An ongoing collaborative alliance among service providers.

Pros:

- Brings together experts on the day-to-day issues
- Allows buy-in of solutions among those who will implement changes

Cons:

- Remains dependent on outside authorities for resources, policy changes, and so forth
- Creates conflict of interest between what is best for community and what is best for each organization's survival
- May become internally focused and lose sight of community goals

(2) Collaboration of Funders

An ongoing collaborative alliance among funders (including local foundations, corporations, United Way, local government, and federal government).

Pros:

- Allows resources to be pooled on behalf of community goal and for use with larger, more complex projects
- Enables funders to be proactive, not reactive
- Reduces administrative burden for nonprofits when funders streamline processes and requirements

Cons:

- May limit engagement with providers and broader community about best solutions
- Comingling funds across sectors can be difficult

(3) Collaboration of Institution Leaders

An ongoing collaborative alliance among professional leaders of various community institutions (hospital, major nonprofit, county offices, education system, justice system, and so on).

Pros:

- Brings together experts on various issues or systems to explore interrelations; gives breadth to community governance
- Allows access to resources within each institution
- Brings authority to implement decisions

Cons:

- Institution structure distances collaboration from citizens
- Authority limited by policies or regulations outside control of members
- Member thinking may be limited by perception that institution regulations cannot be changed

Notes

1   O'Looney, John. (2000). Presentation at the University of Michigan, Interdisciplinary Committee on Organizational Studies, Ann Arbor.

2   See, for example, La Piana, David. (1997). *Beyond Collaboration: Strategic Restructuring of Nonprofit Organizations*. San Francisco: James Irvine Foundation.

3   Hardy, Quentin. (2000, May 1). "The Radical Philanthropist," *Forbes* Online: www.forbes.com/forbes/2000/0501/6510114a_4.html.

4   Quotation from p. 1 of Domanico, Raymond, Carol Innerst, Alexander Russo, Chester E. Finn, Jr., and Marci Kanstoroom. (2000). "Can Philanthropy Fix Our Schools?: Appraising Walter Annenberg's $500 Million Gift to Public Education." Washington, DC: Thomas B. Fordham Foundation.

See also:

Allen, Kent. (2000, April 18). "Philanthropy: Give and Take: Tough Marks for Annenberg Education Grant," *Washington Post*, p. A27.

"Report: Annenberg's $500 Million Schools-Improvement Effort Missed Goals." (2000, April 19). *Philanthropy News Network* Online: www.pnnonline.org.

Sommerfeld, Meg. (2000, May 4). "What Did the Money Buy?" *Chronicle of Philanthropy*, 12(14), pp. 1, 7, 8, 10.

5   *Giving USA 2000*. Indianapolis: American Association of Fundraising Counsel Trust for Philanthropy: www.aafrc.org.

6   See the following:

California Wellness Foundation web site: www.letsgetreal.org; and Communication Sciences Group. (1999). "Solutions: Getting Real About Teen Pregnancy" (online document).

Gallagher, Kaia, and Jodi Drisko. (2000). *Building Community Capacity for Teen Pregnancy Prevention*. Denver: Colorado Trust.

7   Carson, Emmet C. (2000, January 27). "Opinion: Grant Makers Mustn't Hide Behind Trendy Strategies," *Chronicle of Philanthropy*, 12(7), pp. 32–33. (Quotation from page 32.)

8   Weiss, Heather B., and M. Elena Lopez. (2000, Winter). "New Strategies in Foundation Grantmaking for Children and Youth," *Community Youth Development Journal* Online: www.cydjournal.org/2000Winter/weiss.html.

9   Stone, Melissa. (2000, February 18). Presentation at the University of Michigan, Interdisciplinary Committee on Organizational Studies, Ann Arbor, www.si.umich.edu/ICOS/Presentations/20000218/019.htm.

10 Spekman, Robert E., Lynn A. Isabella, and Thomas C. MacAvoy. (2000). *Alliance Competence: Maximizing the Value of Your Partnerships*. New York: John Wiley & Sons, Inc.

11 Pew Partnership for Civic Change and Campaign Study Group. (2001). *Ready Willing and Able: Americans Tackle Their Communities*. Charlottesville, VA: Pew Partnership, published online at www.pew-partnership.org.

12 For more on these approaches to community work, see, for example:

Aspen Roundtable on Comprehensive Community Initiatives. (1997). *Voices from the Field: Learning from the Early Work of Comprehensive Community Initiatives*. Washington, DC: Aspen Institute.

Hess, Douglas R. (1999). "Community Organizing, Building, and Developing: Their Relationship to Comprehensive Community Initiatives." Paper presented on COMM-ORG: The On-Line Conference on Community Organizing and Development: http://comm-org.utoledo.edu/papers.htm.

Pitcoff, Winton. (1998, January/February). "Comprehensive Community Initiatives: Redefining Community Development," *Shelterforce* Online: www.nhi.org.

Potapchuk, William R., and Caroline Polk. (1994). *Building the Collaborative Community.* Washington, DC: National Institute for Dispute Resolution, National Civic League, and Program for Community Problem Solving.

Resources listed online under "Community-Based Strategies" on the Welfare Information Network: www.welfareinfo.org.

Resources listed online at the Community Building Resource Exchange: www.commbuild.org.

[13] Center for the Study of Social Policy. (1995). "Changing Governance to Achieve Better Results for Children and Families." Washington, DC: Child Protection Clearinghouse, CSSP, p. 3.

[14] Annie E. Casey Foundation. (1995). "The Path of Most Resistance: Reflections on Lessons Learned from New Futures." Baltimore: Annie E. Casey Foundation, p. 20.

[15] Angelica, Emil, and Vincent Hyman. (1997). *Coping with Cutbacks: The Nonprofit Guide to Success When Times Are Tight.* St. Paul, MN: Amherst H. Wilder Foundation.

[16] Annie E. Casey Foundation. (1995). "The Path of Most Resistance," pp. 7–8.

[17] The Annie E. Casey Foundation discusses these limitations of lead organizations in its assessment report of its Rebuilding Communities Initiative. See Burns, Tom, and Gerri Spilka. (1997). "The Planning Phase of the Rebuilding Communities Initiative." Baltimore: Annie E. Casey Foundation.

[18] See, for example:

Byrne, John A. (2000, August 28). "Management by Web," *Business Week,* pp. 84–96.

Tedeschi, Bob. (2000, October 2). "E-Commerce Report," *New York Times,* p. C12.

19   Collaboratory for Community Support. (2000). *Management Information Systems for Collaborative Approaches to Homelessness*. Ann Arbor, MI: Collaboratory for Community Support.

20   "Changing Governance to Achieve Better Results for Children and Families," p. 17.

21   Case study drawn from LINC publication: "LINC in Brief"; LINC web site: www.kclinc.org; and interview with Gayle A. Hobbs, executive director, February 2000.

22   See, for example:

Friedman, Mark. (2000). "Reforming Finance, Financing Reform for Family and Children's Services." Sacramento: Foundation Consortium.

Schorr, Lisbeth, Frank Farrow, David Hornbeck, and Sara Watson. (1995). "The Case for Shifting to Results-Based Accountability." Washington, DC: The Improved Outcomes for Children Project, Center for the Study of Social Policy.

United Way of America. (1996). *Measuring Program Outcomes: A Practical Approach*. Alexandria, VA: United Way of America.

23   Greene, Stephen G. (2001, February 22). "Changing Course," *Chronicle of Philanthropy*, 13(9), pp. 10–12. (Quotation from p. 10.)

24   Connor, Joseph A., Chrissa H. Ventrelle, and Stephanie Kadel-Taras. (2000, March/April). "Learning from Funder Collaboratives," *Foundation News & Commentary*, 41(2), pp. 44–47.

25   Case study drawn from LAUF annual reports; SCAP publication: "New Directions for Southern California Philanthropy"; SCAP web site: www.scap.org; and interviews with Elwood Hopkins, LAUF project director, and Maria Grace, assistant project director, July 1999.

26   Schorr, Lisbeth, Kathleen Sylvester, and Margaret Dunkle. (1999). *Strategies to Achieve a Common Purpose: Tools for Turning Good Ideas into Good Policies*. Washington, DC: Institute for Educational Leadership, p. 23. (Available online at www.iel.org/pubs/strategies.html.)

27 Aspen Roundtable on Comprehensive Community Initiatives. (1997). *Voices from the Field: Learning from the Early Work of Comprehensive Community Initiatives.* Washington, DC: Aspen Institute. (Available online at www.aspenroundtable.org/voices/index.htm.)

28 Bruner, Charles. (1996). *Realizing a Vision for Children, Families, and Neighborhoods: An Alternative to Other Modest Proposals.* Des Moines: National Center for Service Integration, p. 51.

29 Spears, Larry C. (Ed.). (1998). *The Power of Servant Leadership: Essays by Robert K. Greenleaf.* San Francisco: Berrett-Koehler.

30 Case study drawn from NCCC web site: www.ncccsf.org, and interview with Ed Schoenberger, NCCC president, January 26, 2000.

31 For two summaries of our work in this area, see:

Connor, J. A., and S. Kadel-Taras. (2000, December). "Organizing Community Work to Reach Solutions," *Philanthropy News Network* Online: www.pnnonline.org.

Connor, J. A., and S. Kadel-Taras. (2000, June). "The Community Support Organization: Linking Not-for-Profits to Community Impact," *Not-for-Profit CEO Monthly Letter*, 7(8), pp. 1–3.

32 For more on the potential benefits and risks of management support organizations serving as CSOs, see Connor, Joseph A., Stephanie Kadel-Taras, and Diane Vinokur-Kaplan. (1999, Winter). "The Role of Nonprofit Management Support Organizations in Sustaining Community Collaborations," *Nonprofit Management and Leadership*, 10(2), pp. 127–136.

33 For more on this idea, see Friedman, Mark. (2000).

34 Thank you to John Tropman, professor, School of Social Work, University of Michigan, for this witty observation.

35 Case study drawn from the Peninsula Community Foundation web site: www.pcf.org; interview with foundation president, Sterling Speirn, February 5, 2001; and interview with Peninsula partnership director, Jennifer Sedbrook, March 14, 2001. For additional resources visit Collaboratory's web site at www.comnet.org/collaboratorycs and see the reading list at www.comnet.org/collaboratorycs/SW697.html.

36 Senge, Peter M., Art Kleiner, Charlotte Roberts, George Roth, Rick Ross, and Bryan Smith. (1999). *The Dance of Change: The Challenges to Sustaining Momentum in Learning Organizations.* New York: Doubleday, p. 45.

Index

fig indicates figures

fig indicates figures

More results-oriented books from the Amherst H. Wilder Foundation

Collaboration

Collaboration Handbook
Creating, Sustaining, and Enjoying the Journey
by Michael Winer and Karen Ray

Shows you how to get a collaboration going, set goals, determine everyone's roles, create an action plan, and evaluate the results. Includes a case study of one collaboration from start to finish, helpful tips on how to avoid pitfalls, and worksheets to keep everyone on track.

192 pages, softcover   Item # 069032

Collaboration: What Makes It Work, 2nd Ed.
by Paul Mattessich, PhD, Marta Murray-Close, BA, and Barbara Monsey, MPH

An in-depth review of current collaboration research. Major findings are summarized, critical conclusions are drawn, and twenty key factors influencing successful collaborations are identified. Includes The Wilder Collaboration Factors Inventory, which groups can use to assess their collaboration.

104 pages, softcover   Item # 069326

The Nimble Collaboration
Fine-Tuning Your Collaboration for Lasting Success
by Karen Ray

Shows you ways to make your existing collaboration more responsive, flexible, and productive. Provides three key strategies to help your collaboration respond quickly to changing environments and participants.

136 pages, softcover   Item # 069288

Funder's Guides

Community Visions, Community Solutions
Grantmaking for Comprehensive Impact
by Joseph A. Connor and Stephanie Kadel-Taras

Helps foundations, community funds, government agencies, and other grantmakers uncover a community's highest aspiration for itself, and support and sustain strategic efforts to get to workable solutions.

128 pages, softcover   Item # 06930X

Strengthening Nonprofit Performance
A Funder's Guide to Capacity Building
Paul Connolly and Carol Lukas

This practical guide synthesizes the most recent capacity building practice and research into a collection of strategies, steps, and examples that you can use to get started on or improve funding to strengthen nonprofit organizations.

176 pages, softcover   Item # 069377

Management & Planning

Benchmarking for Nonprofits
How to Measure, Manage, and Improve Performance
by Jason Saul

Benchmarking—the onging process of measuring your organization against leaders—can help stimulate innovation, increase impact, decrease costs, raise money, inspire staff, impress funders, engage your board, and sharpen your mission. This book defines a systematic and reliable way to benchmark, from preparing your organization to measuring performance and implementing best practices.

112 pages, softcover   Item # 069431

The Best of the Board Café
Hands-on Solutions for Nonprofit Boards
by Jan Masaoka, CompassPoint Nonprofit Services

Gathers the most requested articles from the e-newsletter, *Board Café.* You'll find a lively menu of ideas, information, opinions, news, and resources to help board members give and get the most out of their board service.

232 pages, softcover   Item # 069407

Bookkeeping Basics
What Every Nonprofit Bookkeeper Needs to Know
by Debra L. Ruegg and Lisa M. Venkatrathnam

Complete with step-by-step instructions, a glossary of accounting terms, detailed examples, and handy reproducible forms, this book will enable you to successfully meet the basic bookkeeping requirements of your nonprofit organization—even if you have little or no formal accounting training.

128 pages, softcover   Item # 069296

For current prices or to order visit us online at 🖥 www.wilder.org/pubs

Consulting with Nonprofits
A Practitioner's Guide
by Carol A. Lukas

A step-by-step, comprehensive guide for consultants. Addresses the art of consulting, how to run your business, and much more. Also includes tips and anecdotes from thirty skilled consultants.

240 pages, softcover   Item # 069172

The Wilder Nonprofit Field Guide to
Crafting Effective Mission and Vision Statements
by Emil Angelica

Guides you through two six-step processes that result in a mission statement, vision statement, or both. Shows how a clarified mission and vision lead to more effective leadership, decisions, fundraising, and management. Includes tips, sample statements, and worksheets.

88 pages, softcover   Item # 06927X

The Wilder Nonprofit Field Guide to
Developing Effective Teams
by Beth Gilbertsen and Vijit Ramchandani

Helps you understand, start, and maintain a team. Provides tools and techniques for writing a mission statement, setting goals, conducting effective meetings, creating ground rules to manage team dynamics, making decisions in teams, creating project plans, and developing team spirit.

80 pages, softcover   Item # 069202

The Five Life Stages of Nonprofit Organizations
Where You Are, Where You're Going, and What to Expect When You Get There
by Judith Sharken Simon with J. Terence Donovan

Shows you what's "normal" for each development stage which helps you plan for transitions, stay on track, and avoid unnecessary struggles. Includes The Wilder Nonprofit Life Stage Assessment to plot your organization's progress in seven arenas of organization development.

128 pages, softcover   Item # 069229

The Lobbying and Advocacy Handbook for Nonprofit Organizations
Shaping Public Policy at the State and Local Level
by Marcia Avner

The Lobbying and Advocacy Handbook is a planning guide and resource for nonprofit organizations that want to influence issues that matter to them. This book will help you decide whether to lobby and then put plans in place to make it work.

240 pages, softcover   Item # 069261

The Manager's Guide to Program Evaluation:
Planning, Contracting, and Managing for Useful Results
by Paul W. Mattessich, Ph.D.

Explains how to plan and manage an evaluation that will help identify your organization's successes, share information with key audiences, and improve services.

96 pages, softcover   Item # 069385

The Nonprofit Board Member's Guide to Lobbying and Advocacy
by Marcia Avner

Written specifically for board members, this guide helps organizations increase their impact on policy decisions. It reveals how board members can be involved in planning for and implementing successful lobbying efforts.

96 pages, softcover   Item # 069393

The Nonprofit Mergers Workbook
The Leader's Guide to Considering, Negotiating, and Executing a Merger
by David La Piana

A merger can be a daunting and complex process. Save time, money, and untold frustration with this highly practical guide that makes the process manageable and controllable. Includes case studies, decision trees, twenty-two worksheets, checklists, tips, and complete step-by-step guidance from seeking partners to writing the merger agreement, and more.

240 pages, softcover   Item # 069210

The Nonprofit Mergers Workbook Part II
Unifying the Organization after a Merger
by La Piana Associates

Once the merger agreement is signed, the question becomes: How do we make this merger work? *Part II* helps you create a comprehensive plan to achieve *integration*—bringing together people, programs, processes, and systems from two (or more) organizations into a single, unified whole.

248 pages, includes CD-ROM   Item # 069415

Nonprofit Stewardship
A Better Way to Lead Your Mission-Based Organization
by Peter C. Brinckerhoff

You may lead a not-for-profit organization, but it's not your organization. It belongs to the community it serves. You are the steward—the manager of resources that belong to someone else. The stewardship model of leadership can help your organization improve its mission capability by forcing you to keep your organization's mission foremost. It helps you make decisions that are best for the people your organization serves. In other words, stewardship helps you do more good for more people.

272 pages, softcover   Item # 069423

Resolving Conflict in Nonprofit Organizations
The Leader's Guide to Finding Constructive Solutions
by Marion Peters Angelica

Helps you identify conflict, decide whether to intervene, uncover and deal with the true issues, and design and conduct a conflict resolution process. Includes exercises to learn and practice conflict resolution skills, guidance on handling unique conflicts such as harassment and discrimination, and when (and where) to seek outside help with litigation, arbitration, and mediation.

192 pages, softcover   Item # 069164

Strategic Planning Workbook for Nonprofit Organizations, Revised and Updated
by Bryan Barry

Chart a wise course for your nonprofit's future. This time-tested workbook gives you practical step-by-step guidance, real-life examples, one nonprofit's complete strategic plan, and easy-to-use worksheets.

144 pages, softcover   Item # 069075

Marketing & Fundraising

The Wilder Nonprofit Field Guide to
Conducting Successful Focus Groups
by Judith Sharken Simon

Shows how to collect valuable information without a lot of money or special expertise. Using this proven technique, you'll get essential opinions and feedback to help you check out your assumptions, do better strategic planning, improve services or products, and more.

80 pages, softcover   Item # 069199

Coping with Cutbacks:
The Nonprofit Guide to Success When Times Are Tight
by Emil Angelica and Vincent Hyman

Shows you practical ways to involve business, government, and other nonprofits to solve problems together. Also includes 185 cutback strategies you can put to use right away.

128 pages, softcover   Item # 069091

The Wilder Nonprofit Field Guide to
Fundraising on the Internet
by Gary M. Grobman, Gary B. Grant, and Steve Roller

Your quick road map to using the Internet for fundraising. Shows you how to attract new donors, troll for grants, get listed on sites that assist donors, and learn more about the art of fundraising. Includes detailed reviews of 77 web sites useful to fundraisers, including foundations, charities, prospect research sites, and sites that assist donors.

64 pages, softcover   Item # 069180

Marketing Workbook for Nonprofit Organizations Volume I: Develop the Plan
by Gary J. Stern

Don't just wish for results—get them! Here's how to create a straightforward, usable marketing plan. Includes the six Ps of Marketing, how to use them effectively, a sample marketing plan, tips on using the Internet, and worksheets.

208 pages, softcover   Item # 069253

For current prices, a catalog, or to order call 800-274-6024

Marketing Workbook for Nonprofit Organizations Volume II: Mobilize People for Marketing Success
by Gary J. Stern

Put together a successful promotional campaign based on the most persuasive tool of all: personal contact. Learn how to mobilize your entire organization, its staff, volunteers, and supporters in a focused, one-to-one marketing campaign. Comes with *Pocket Guide for Marketing Representatives*. In it, your marketing representatives can record key campaign messages and find motivational reminders.

192 pages, softcover   Item # 069105

Venture Forth! The Essential Guide to Starting a Moneymaking Business in Your Nonprofit Organization
by Rolfe Larson

The most complete guide on nonprofit business development. Building on the experience of dozens of organizations, this handbook gives you a time-tested approach for finding, testing, and launching a successful nonprofit business venture.

272 pages, softcover   Item # 069245

Vital Communities

Community Building: What Makes It Work
by Wilder Research Center

Reveals twenty-eight keys to help you build community more effectively. Includes detailed descriptions of each factor, case examples of how they play out, and practical questions to assess your work.

112 pages, softcover   Item # 069121

Community Economic Development Handbook
by Mihailo Temali

A concrete, practical handbook to turning any neighborhood around. It explains how to start a community economic development organization, and then lays out the steps of four proven and powerful strategies for revitalizing inner-city neighborhoods.

288 pages, softcover   Item # 069369

The Wilder Nonprofit Field Guide to
Conducting Community Forums
by Carol Lukas and Linda Hoskins

Provides step-by-step instruction to plan and carry out exciting, successful community forums that will educate the public, build consensus, focus action, or influence policy.

128 pages, softcover   Item # 069318

Violence Prevention & Intervention

The Little Book of Peace
24 pages (minimum order 10 copies)   Item # 069083
*Also available in **Spanish** and **Hmong** language editions.*

Journey Beyond Abuse: A Step-by-Step Guide to Facilitating Women's Domestic Abuse Groups.
208 pages, softcover   Item # 069148

Moving Beyond Abuse: Stories and Questions for Women Who Have Lived with Abuse
(Companion guided journal to *Journey Beyond Abuse*)
88 pages, softcover   Item # 069156

Foundations for Violence-Free Living:
A Step-by-Step Guide to Facilitating Men's Domestic Abuse Groups
240 pages, softcover   Item # 069059

On the Level
(Participant's workbook to *Foundations for Violence-Free Living*)
160 pages, softcover   Item # 069067

What Works in Preventing Rural Violence
by Wilder Research Center
94 pages, softcover   Item # 069040

ORDERING INFORMATION

Order by phone, fax or online

Call toll-free: 800-274-6024
Internationally: 651-659-6024

Fax: 651-642-2061

E-mail: books@wilder.org
Online: www.wilder.org/pubs

Mail: Amherst H. Wilder Foundation
Publishing Center
919 Lafond Avenue
St. Paul, MN 55104

Our NO-RISK guarantee

If you aren't completely satisfied with any book for any reason, simply send it back within 30 days for a full refund.

Pricing and discounts

For current prices and discounts, please visit our web site at www.wilder.org/pubs or call toll free at 800-274-6024.

Do you have a book idea?

Wilder Publishing Center seeks manuscripts and proposals for books in the fields of nonprofit management and community development. To get a copy of our author guidelines, please call us at 800-274-6024. You can also download them from our web site at www.wilder.org/pubs/author_guide.html.

Visit us online

You'll find information about the Wilder Foundation and more details on our books, such as table of contents, pricing, discounts, endorsements, and more, at www.wilder.org/pubs.

Quality assurance

We strive to make sure that all the books we publish are helpful and easy to use. Our major workbooks are tested and critiqued by experts before being published. Their comments help shape the final book and—we trust—make it more useful to you.